Making a Movement

With the Disruptors Driving Social Change Around the World

Barney Cullum

Acropolis

First published by Acropolis Publishing, a division of Canbury Press Ltd 2023

This edition published 2023

Canbury Press

Kingston upon Thames, Surrey, United Kingdom

www.canburypress.com

Printed and bound in Great Britain

Typeset in Athelas (body), Futura PT (headings)

This is a work of non-fiction

ISBN:

Paperback 9781914487309

Ebook 9781914487316

CONTENTS

Contents

Contents

An Extinction Rebellion protest in October 2023. © Barney Cullum

INTRODUCTION:
THE DISRUPTORS' DECADE

May 2023 and I'm due to attend 'nonviolence training' in London. The preparation-for-protest session represents an opportunity for me to see how Just Stop Oil operate in person.

Just Stop Oil – 'a coalition of groups working together to influence the government to commit to halting new fossil fuel licensing and production' – have generated blanket media coverage during the first few months of the year.

I receive a press release from them at least once a day. It's more contact than I receive from any other protest group.

The coverage this coalition receives in the mainstream press is mixed, often negative. But Just Stop Oil are racking up headlines in line with their strategy. Typically, they cover high-profile sports events, theatre productions, art galleries and the like in orange powder or paint to make their point.

From Wimbledon to the World Snooker Championships, the full spectrum of UK sporting events has been humbled – or should that be Tangoed – by their luminous protests.

As a result, Just Stop Oil report credibly that their 'brand recognition' has soared to 92 per cent: more than nine in ten surveyed know who they are and what they stand for. That's far higher than the numbers achieved by Greenpeace, arguably their ideological grandfathers, with whom they share an affinity for media-genic 'shock and awe' demonstrations. And Just Stop Oil only got going in 2022.

From politicians to the public, they are now on everyone's radar. Their tactics are necessarily disruptive, for they are following civil disobedience approaches which demand their actions to be just that. They stage more than satsuma-coloured stunts. The old-fashioned march became their bread and butter in the summer of 2023, with daily walks slowing traffic across the capital again in autumn.

Enemies have been made, perhaps in the millions. But donations have been on that scale, too, with regular one-off appeals attracting public funding of a volume traditional A-list charities, also starved of government funding, can only dream of.

Just Stop Oil's online introductions have been as friendly and welcoming in their interactive sections as they are slick and persuasive in their storytelling. In May 2023, I'm thinking I'll know them far better once I've showed up for in-person training.

Ultimately, however, I don't go. On the eve of the King's coronation the Home Secretary, Suella Braverman, unilaterally changes British protest law by the back door. She downgrades the legal definition of 'serious disruption' in the Public Order Act 1986 to merely 'more than minor'. This gives police almost unlimited power to shut down protests and criminalise those taking part.

The change has previously been rejected by Parliament when the government tried to insert it into the Public Order Act 2023. But Braverman introduces it using a statutory instrument: a form of secondary legislation created by ministers to override Parliament. As the rights group Liberty described in mounting their legal challenge against Braverman's intervention, statutory instruments get much less time for scrutiny and debate by elected MPs. And they can never be amended.

Use of statutory instruments is becoming increasingly common in British Parliament, with profound consequences for democracy and protest. And for now, the right to protest, in effect, has been criminalised.

The change stops me from attending Just Stop Oil's training – even though I would have been there purely for research. Several protesters on Just Stop Oil slow marches have been arrested since the law was re-written – by a solitary politician.

Braverman's act is bad news for protest, but it is bad news for politics and conventional campaigning, too. And that has implications for policy and practice across all dimensions of our social landscape.

The UK faces a crossroads. Anyone concerned with, involved in, or curious about community organising, at any level and in any format – whether that's voluntary campaigning, charity organising, politics or any form of citizen activism at all – feels this crossroads we have arrived at.

We have arrived at a place that threatens what we have considered to be the fundamentals of democracy and freedom. Encouragingly, we are seeing rising energy, values, principles and creativity across grassroots social movements.

How are we defining social movements in these pages? Any push for change led and organised by ordinary people; societies, communities, organisations or groups.

Love them or loathe them, Just Stop Oil have demonstrated remarkable skill in mobilising, funding and creatively raising awareness of their cause. But their work, building on the foundations laid by Extinction Rebellion, is just one manifestation of a wave of activism that has swept across causes and geographies in the past decade.

2023 also marked ten years of Black Lives Matter, now a transcendent global network.

2024 is anticipated to be an election year in Great Britain. But ten years on from Hong Kong's Umbrella Movement, there remains no universal suffrage there. Things are sunnier in Taiwan, which will celebrate ten years since 1,000 students occupied parliament to defy an imminent pact with China.

The time to reflect on the tactics and achievements of all the new forms of activism we've seen over the last ten years is now. In 2023, protesters in Israel took to the streets in their tens and sometimes hundreds of thousands every Saturday night to rail against corruption. In Sweden, 2023 marked the five-year anniversary of the school strikes for climate protests. Greta Thunberg, who started the 'school strike for climate' protests in 2018, faced court for the first time. Some of her peers, now in their early twenties, graduated in law and crowdfunded to sue the state over its inaction on emissions.

I regret having to miss the non-violent training delivered by Just Stop Oil in London. But in researching this book I met with the group's founder, Roger Hallam, interviewing him from his hospital bed. I also joined the protests in Israel and Sweden. And I caught up with the leader of Black Lives Matter about the vital and groundbreaking changes they've driven. As with most movements, the precious impacts achieved and the behind-the-scenes tactics followed have been less well documented to date than the associated protests.

Elsewhere I have met and quizzed activists, lawyers, political scientists, campaigners, graffiti artists, anthropologists, peace-builders, hactivists, charity directors, authors, Olympians, refugees, researchers and every other kind of change agent you can imagine. From every corner of the world. For this book. Because now is the time to learn, share, defend and apply the lessons of the eruption of social change disruption we've experienced over the past decade.

PART ONE

REBELS' WORLD – ENVIRONMENTALIST IMAGINATION AND RESISTANCE

CHAPTER ONE
EXTINCTION REBELLION AND JUST STOP OIL – DIVISIVE CONQUESTS

I interview Roger Hallam, the Extinction Rebellion co-founder, from his hospital bed. It is the first day of XR's self described 'Big One'. The environmental activists have mobilised a record 60,000 people in London for its first non-disruptive demonstration, a temporary change in tactics introduced in spring 2023 to incentivise more people to join the global movement.

I had been intending to meet Hallam in the thick of things in Parliament Square, but a cycling accident shifts our interview to Zoom instead. I had originally been given a ten-minute slot at 1 o'clock but there is no-one there when I open the call.

His assistant wakes him on my behalf to remind him of the appointment. I only learn of his accident when he dials in. Hallam apologises for having fallen asleep then pivots his laptop to show me his right leg, enmeshed in an external fixator. The medical equipment is holding several broken bones in place.

It's ironic that an accident endured while using climate-friendly transport has denied him the prospect of attending the Big One.

While XR have distanced themselves from their founder in recent years, it was Hallam that laid the blueprint for today's public descent on the capital. It's all mapped out in Chapter 14, 'The Civil Resistance Model', of the XR handbook *This is Not a Drill*, published four years earlier in 2019.

Medical drowsiness does not prevent a characteristically straight-talking opening salvo from the 56-year-old. 'The indigenous activists in Canada that I've had long conversations with have the choice of doing nothing and dying [due to the climate emergency], or resisting and dying. So I suggest you state the obvious at the start of your write-up so that you don't pre-frame this as some kind of interesting little campaign.

> There's a real world out there and if you participate in the promotion of the greatest conceit in human history [denial of the climate emergency] you will find yourself in the court because the next generation are not going to be post-modernist – spending all their lives putting their fingers in dykes – because you fucked up... because our generation fucked up.
>
> And it's human nature that they will come after you in various ways. As long as our generation abdicates its responsibility the more we end up looking like the Germans in the 1930s. If you 'do them in', its human nature that they'll come and 'do you in' later.

It's direct talking from the man behind modern direct action. It's also a very different tone than that which has been struck earlier in the morning at the Big One's opening ceremony. I'd watched from the front row at 11am as Clare Farrell, a fellow activist who conceived XR alongside Hallam in a pub in Stroud in England's south west a decade ago, took to the portable stage. From a small raised platform, she eulogised her new found faith in the potentially transformative role of 'love' and 'coalition'.

Farrell, for now at least, was persuaded that these new tactics best supported XR's prospects of winning its argument for the government to reduce greenhouse gas emissions to net zero by 2025 and to create and be led by citizens' assemblies.

'In the history of the UK, I don't think there have ever been so many groups committed to working together, to ongoing collaboration,' Farrell tells activists and members of an 80-strong coalition of charities and campaign group. 'This is not just a march, a demonstration or a protest, this is the beginning of a new era of solidarity and support and determination.'

This moment draws the biggest cheer from Farrell's five-minute speech, but the occasion, opened with an incongruous reference to the 'typical British weather' lacks Hallam's urgency. His is a confrontational spirit that, though divisive, drove environmentalism higher and faster up the agenda than any previous tactics in the United Kingdom.

Hallam has a PhD in Civil Resistance, obtained from King's College London. The Welsh firebrand and former farmer lived out of his car while completing his thesis in the capital. He turned to academia for answers on delivering social change after farming became unsustainable due to climate breakdown.

While XR dabbles with less confrontational demonstrations, Hallam has gone on to form two further direct action groups that have positioned themselves as even more adversarial and creative than the original carnation of XR. Insulate Britain, the first, has been followed by Just Stop Oil.

While all three organisations have attracted legions of critics, Hallam's fire and artistry have also drawn legions of loyal footsoldiers prepared to face prison for the cause.

The protesters now joining Just Stop Oil's slick, persuasive and welcoming online and in-person trainings sessions are markedly younger than the typical profiles of XR meet-ups today, where the median age is higher than it was.

George Hibberd, a 30-year-old airline pilot, was among the first to be arrested in the name of Just Stop Oil. Hibberd was prosecuted alongside 20 others protesters who glued themselves to the road outside Harrods, the luxury London department store, after spray-painting the building orange.

'Our demand is for the government to agree no new oil or gas licenses,' Hibberd tells me in between co-ordinating a two-week slow march campaign that will commence the day after the 96-hour Big One concludes. 'This is a no-brainer demand.' He says:

> We closed down oil terminals for two weeks but the media barely covered it. It didn't achieve much so we decided to change tactics towards direct actions. We organised protests at the BAFTAs [an entertainment awards show]; we threw soups at paintings [Vincent Van Gogh's Sunflowers at London's National Gallery has featured among the art work targeted]; we disrupted football matches. All of these are more uncomfortable for us as supporters of Just Stop Oil, because it's not nice for us to be disrupting the public.

> However all political parties – other than the Conservatives – have signed up to our demand. NatWest have also agreed to stop funding fossil fuels: a massive win.

Achieving cross-party consensus, other than with the Conservatives, on no more oil and gas licenses is a major win. This cross-party consensus has followed [from shifting] public opinion. Despite media ridicule, we've achieved a fair amount.

We have to keep pushing, finding the sweet-spot from a lot of public facing actions that create media attention, start conversations and apply pressure.

The UK is quite different to some European countries that objectively are more progressive, with more of a free press and free media. Here, all of our newspapers are owned by five billionaires. Our TV media are basically run by New Labour. Neither of those are amenable to the left point [of view].

What we have is virtual media silence on the issue and the only way we get media... our hand is forced to do these public facing actions. It forces people to watch our protests.

A day before we speak, a Just Stop Oil protester has just forced the postponement of the 2023 World Snooker Championship. 25-year-old Eddie Whittingham joined Margaret Reid, 52, in racing from the theatre seats to turn the green baize of the snooker table into the bright orange that has become synonymous with the group's actions. Similar stunts were pulled throughout the summer at high-profile rugby and golf events and the Wimbledon Tennis Championships.

'Protests like that provoke conversations. People ask, why did he do that, my friend from Exeter University? Often it gets people to talk about the issue at hand.'

'We're not doing this to "win"; we're doing this because it's the right thing to do. We are driven by values and purpose.'

Protesters, police and politicians alike are all now doubling down. A public order bill brought in on the eve of the coronation of King Charles coincided with the daily slow marches George had been organising.

Dozens were arrested in the first fortnights of the protests. 'We're looking to create a dilemma,' Hibberd explains. 'We're asking people to get involved in the slow-marches and our key message for this campaign is – in addition to ending oil and gas – we're asking people in power to pick a side.'

Reflecting on the scale of the mobilisation at the Big One and the tactics carried out by Just Stop Oil, we're reminded again that Britain's non-violent climate activists are carrying out the six-point plan laid out by Hallam in *This is Not a Drill*, the XR handbook.

- First, you need the numbers, ideally 50,000.
- You have to go to the capital city, that is where the government is, that is where the elites hang out.
- You have to break the law... because it creates the social tension and the public drama which are vital to create change.
- It has to stay non-violent.
- It has to go on day after day.
- Last but not least, it has to be fun. The artistic communities need to be on board. We are going to show the media that we are not sitting around waiting to die any longer.

Hallam, writing in 2019, predicts a repressive backlash – which plays out with three new laws passed in quick succession lowering the arrest threshold for protest – and foretells how this will trigger a counter-response of greater mobilisation of protesters.

I pick this up with Hallam during our interview. We are continuing virtually, from his hospital bed, into a second hour. But the webcam confirms there are plenty of grapes in shot.

> Transgressive action is effective on two levels. The first is that it's objectively effective because – per unit of labour-put-in – it produces a massive social effect. Initially, this is in terms of public order and negative publicity. In the medium-long term, it produces social change having resisted it. Not every time of course – but it's a lot more effective than what you might call 'conventional campaigning'.

> That's the external effects. The other interesting thing in this is the internal effects because transgressive actions can emotionally galvanise people in so much as people are drawn to morally good action; people are drawn to social conflict. We're all involuntarily beings that still have feelings of solidarity when people of our own demographic culture are put in harm's way, so social conflict is a significant mechanism for mobilising people.

Hallam adds that the 'micro-design' of organisation and recruitment has been key to the success of his groups, Just Stop Oil, XR and Insulate Britain. 'Micro-design has been completely ignored, to its great detriment, by progressive and radical movements.' You have to build self-feedback mechanisms into all meetings. Even a small change in the initial conditions of co-productivity will mathematically – over time – create a mass movement, as opposed to six Marxists back in a pub, which is what most movements degenerate into.'

In our interview Hallam name checks Martin Luther King and Mahatma Gandhi to back up his faith in civil disobedience working again. The 56-year-old does this despite his awareness that critics regard this as historical determinism, that history never repeats itself:

> People will look back at [the direct actions of XR and Just Stop Oil] as the initial manifestations, the initial flare-ups because these things are all intrinsic.
>
> It's not like suddenly one day everything changes. A good five or so years before anything major happens you always get flare-ups, right? You might get riots, you might get civil disobedience movements. You look at Gandhi and 1960 and then also before the non-violent campaign – well, how that's seen now is that the 1940s saw the big precursor campaigns.
>
> If you're a vulgar Marxist, you'll say it's a law of history that historical determinism has been proven to be lacking, to put it mildly. However no-one is doubting *physical* determinism in the sense that you know, if I get gangrene in my leg next week, it's previously been determined that I'll have to have it cut off, right? That's the way it is.
>
> The point is this thing [the climate emergency] is now locked-in as a physical crisis. These physical activities are now locked-in, due to putting carbon into the atmosphere, to 420 parts to the million.
>
> That enables you to give a high level of predictive solidity around what will happen and that predicted activity of course is that revolutionary activities in the widest sense of the word will happen in western society in the next twenty years."

That is close to being an inevitability and it covers a multitude of sins. It could be social collapse, it could be fascism, it could be a re-configuration of 21st Century democracy – but what we do know is that present neo-liberal regimes will not last in their present form, which in the wider scheme of history isn't unusual because regimes never last. Everyone thinks they last forever but they never do, it's just a historical fact.

While the UK has lowered the arrest threshold for protests, at the time of writing the country has yet to see the counter-repression protests on a scale in the 'ew thousands' Hallam believes are needed for the court system to collapse under the weight of administrative pressure.

However the slow marches have correlated with the introduction to parliament of a climate and ecology bill that stands to legislate for 'citizens' assemblies' to shape future environmental policy, one of the primary goals of XR, a movement – lest we forget – that emerged barely five years ago.

'In 2016, environment concerns were number 13 in the whole list of concerns for British people,' Dr Nick Anim, an environmental and social justice programme designer, informs me. 'Come 2019 these concerns ranked second and they've maintained that position throughout the years since. That is because of the work of XR alone.' At the time of our interview, conducted in summer 2023, climate change and the environment featured third among Brits' concerns, behind the economy and inflation, in the 'Issues Index' published by pollsters Ipsos. He says:

"Of course we should recognise the contribution of other movements, such as Fridays for Future – the students who miss school on Fridays to raise awareness of the cause – but these movements have declined. [We'll look at the Fridays for Future movement in the next chapter.] The way XR has managed to take the place... the attention 'marketplace' of the public is by using imaginative tactics, repertoires, a kaleidoscope of disruptive actions.

This drew me to the movement in the first place and I joined XR in April 2019. I was just blown away – everything about it was about creativity.

I was the only black face in most of those spaces but I thought: I've got to be in this game; I've got to stick around; I've got to make sure that the concerns of people like me are put on the table and kept on the table.

When we are forced to look at the history of climate change and how did it start, we are forced to look at the geographies of climate spread and we see that – ah, look – it's an unequal spread of disproportionate impact. These countries that have contributed the least are now asking the bare minimum just to adapt. To adapt! To the catastrophe that they are facing now, we are not talking about the future.

There are generally speaking two XR rebellions every year, one in April and one in September or October. From the pink boat to the occupation of the bank to the Big One, everything XR has done has been mind blowing in terms of unleashing the imagination.

Imagination is absolutely central and there's a lot to learn from that for other movements about how to use imaginative tactics to gain a space and the attention marketplace of the press or the government or the general public – it's the symbiotic relationship of all three because any movement needs support in terms of people and the way to do that is to use imagination, I think.

We need both imagination and rebellion. I am an optimistic person – I wouldn't be an activist if I wasn't – but we need to keep the struggle up. We can't just say there's a climate emergency or accept a bill [if it calls for] reaching net zero carbon emissions by 2050. What you want to talk about is 'really zero'. Net zero just exports our entropy, our winds and so forth, our manufacturing... again, where? Developing countries.

XR's temporary pause in public disruptions is to get as many people on board because of course public disruptions come with the activists' dilemma: While public disruptions will get you coverage in the news for a certain while, they also alienate some people within the public who might agree with your cause but disagree with your approaches to raising awareness about the cause.

So this pause is supposed to try and get as many people on board. It's a radical departure for XR because part of XR's brand is about disruption. It's about creative use of public spaces. It's about creative use of disruption to gain the attention of the public and the press.

think the pause is good in terms of public disruptions [but] I don't think we should necessarily pause disruptions in terms of government institutions and multi-national corporations that have perpetuated these crimes.

We should still bring attention to bear on them. We know from our 2003 Iraq war march that despite the number of people coming on to the streets, the government are still beholden to GDP i.e. the multinational corporations that are lobbying and pushing for their ways of pleasing their shareholders, so we know that [marches alone] necessarily won't cut it.

Ultimately what we need to do in that respect is try to reclaim democracy, which is where the demand for citizens' assemblies comes in – participatory democracy; deliberative democracy. If we wait for the government it will be too little, too late. Informed people can make better judgements.

Again, we must come with imagination. When you hold visionary exercises in the community and say okay, rid yourself of all these things you think are impossible, one of the problems we have found – as a researcher this is what I look at – is even when you ask people to picture 2050 or 2100 and everything being 'sorted', what does the world look like? Still, people are tethered to a certain way of thinking.

It's still hard-core neo-liberal capitalism in their mind (laughs). We need both rebellion *and* imagination. It's an ecosystem, isn't it? It's an ecosystem of change.

CHAPTER TWO

FRIDAYS FOR FUTURE – THE SCHOOL STRIKERS THAT STUDIED HOW TO SUE SWEDEN

Greta Thunberg – save for some eye-catching white Doc Martens – is performing a low-key background role today. It's August 2023 and I'm here to see the first climate action the introvert activist has attended outside Sweden's parliament since the five year anniversary of her first 'school strike for the climate'.

Recently graduated from secondary school – a year later than her peers – Thunberg can no longer call herself a student protester. But she's pledged to keep 'striking' on Fridays. Today represents the first event of the new school year. Thunberg and around twenty others from the Fridays for Future movement are back in front of the Riksdag, quietly continuing their work.

Thunberg has assumed the role of informal communications officer today, filming and live-streaming speeches delivered by travelling environmental activists from Kenya. 'You should speak to them,"'Greta encourages me.

I have already taken the opportunity. Rahmina Paullete, three years Greta's junior, is another precociously talented advocate. The 17-year-old represented Kenya at the COP26 climate summit in Glasgow in 2021 and within a year world leaders had agreed to pay landmark "'oss and damage' reparations to Kenya and other members of the 'G77', a United Nations coalition made up of 134 developing countries.

Paulette tells me her family was forced to flee Mfangano Island for the Kenyan mainland when she was five years old while friends and relatives were left stranded and suffering from lethal impacts of the climate emergency. 'Some did not make it out alive – they died from flooding or water pollution,' Paullete says.

> Some of them are still left there. They're an amazing place, the islands. But problems come from floods and there is poor water sanitation also. Over there, people mainly drink water from the lake directly because [sanitation] is very expensive. So you find that many contract diseases because of the pollution in the lake.

> Some people died because of the pollution and some people died because of the floods. But I want to change my story and impact someone else's life, especially the kids in Europe. Most of them are not being taught what is happening worldwide. They only chat about the European perspective. But once they start listening to the voices that are impacted the most, they can start feeling motivated to work together with us.

It is voices such as Paullete's that Thunberg is increasingly seeking to amplify, those of the people fighting on the front-lines. The Kenyan is a conservationist for Fridays for Future, the movement established by Thunberg. Paullete is also lead campaigner for a separate mission serving her region of Kisumu in Kenya. It's named 'Let Lake Victoria Breathe Again':

> We know Lake Victoria as our home and we don't want to die. I'm trying to relieve the childhoods of many others. The drastic changes of the Lake Victoria region have affected our economy and they also affect us socially, since a lot of us are suffering from climate anxiety.

> We used to go to the lake to feel the breeze but right now no one can go there as there is effluence from the sewage and the chemicals that have been exploited.

> It's really important that climate-induced migrants are present here in Europe because we need a global solidarity where people, especially from the European perspective, are able to share our ideas and push for more implementations. Not only the European Union, but also the United Nations.

> It is so important that youths come together to declare 'climate emergency', especially when it comes to ecosystems that are fragile. We are from Africa, which is one of the continents that emits less, yet we suffer a lot from the impacts of the climate crisis.

Fridays for Future has arguably achieved its biggest policy wins since more international activists from the global south joined the movement.

'We were really excited that the loss and damage compensation commitment got passed,' Paullete says. 'Now we're looking forward, to see if the climate reparations can also be paid back to the community.'

I ask Paullete how her advocacy aimed at the United Nations is making inroads. Thunberg had previously concluded that the COP summits represented opportunities for little more than 'green-washing, lying and cheating'. She says:

> With all our campaigning work, MAPA – MAPA is 'most affected people in areas' – the global south have really tried to strengthen ourselves, working with others globally. Some people are working on policy; some people are working on community-influencing. All of us, with our global south voices, have created more pressure.

> Public facing activism is not enough. So through our activism we looked to influence more negotiators. Most of the time child activists from affected areas are not heard, not given a seat at the table. So we pushed the negotiators to at least hear us, to hear us clarify what we need and what we demand. It has been a struggle but delivering that clarification to the negotiators was really important.

Raquel Frescia, a Peruvian activist, says students from around the world flocked to Fridays for Future having previously been shut down by older generations or the media environment in which they lived:

> For a long time, young people had felt so powerless. The feeling had just been 'my government is so corrupt'. Politicians spoke about the climate in countries like Peru but no-one ever did anything to address it. But then seeing

individuals in Sweden – young individuals – taking action was super inspiring for everyone.

I live in Sweden now but when I go back to Peru, people have somehow heard of Greta and her work and that's amazing. Young people don't know where to put their thoughts and not a lot of young people were really talking about the climate before. Now there is a lot more attention around it and a lot more validation for your opinions on the climate. It gives a safer space. Not only within Fridays for Future, but also around the world more broadly.

Frescia attends the demonstrations outside the Swedish parliament every single Friday. She says she keeps going despite the demands of day to day life – Frescia has attended her driving test earlier on the morning of the day of our interview – to accelerate public awareness of the Fridays for Future cause within the public and with businesses. She shows up for this, rather than out of any faith in influencing the nation's politicians as they walk by.

'Our biggest achievement has been the awareness we have raised in ordinary citizens since we started five years ago. We have people from businesses and the finance sector coming to us and saying "we can't support you publicly because we will get fired, but tell us what we can do to help from the inside". That continues to inspire us.'

'Recently we had a forestation company pledge to fund the Sami movement in Sweden after we spoke to them about the concerns of the Sami people.' The indigenous population of Sweden is one of the groups most threatened by sustainability challenges. 'These are the types of impacts we have seen at Fridays for Future, but when it comes to the politicians, we certainly don't ever think that our politicians are doing enough in response.'

The commitment shown by 'veteran' Fridays for Future activists like Frescia comes at a cost. For the last three years, university students have seen their student loans blocked after attending actions.

New Swedish student groups are organising and fighting back, however. Aurora, an organisation of 600 members, is currently causing their government the most headaches.

Aurora is suing the Swedish state, arguing it has taken insufficient action on emissions to safeguard the prospects of the younger generation.

'In such a dire situation, we need to use every legitimate tool available to us in order to secure sufficient action, sufficiently fast,' says Ida Edling, Aurora's legal and scientific co-ordinator. 'We decided to use law as a tool because it is "un-ignorable".'

Aurora is following where legal activists from the Netherlands, France and Germany have already enjoyed success in holding governments to account on their climate policies.

'We were immensely frustrated with the fact our government and our elected leaders are not doing enough, not taking their responsibility to mitigate the climate crisis.'

While the approach is confrontational, Edling believes strategic litigation can also provide a liberating sense of direction for governments contending with divided electorates.

'I've heard some sources within the government in the Netherlands express relief after receiving a verdict. This was because then they had something to refer to when they took climate actions that were not comfortable for everyone. So I think a verdict can make it easier for politicians to take specific actions.'

'We were very inspired by the case in the Netherlands, where the supreme court issued a final verdict in 2019 saying that the state needed to reduce their climate emissions by 25 per cent by 2020, compared to 1990 levels.' Prior to the case, the government had been working to a target of 17 per cent.

'Similar verdicts have since been issued by high courts in France and Germany. All of these verdicts are based on the European convention of human rights and that is what we are also basing our claims on. This is about making the Swedish state carry out its fair share of the global measures necessary for global warming to be kept below 1.5 degrees, compared to pre-industrial levels.

'As we are building on earlier precedents and using similar arguments, we have great cause for hope that we might also succeed. But we are also adding our own aspects to the case, which is something all climate cases are doing in joining the global climate movement. Everyone is bringing something new and so are we.'

Edling graduated from occasional school strikes to passing her legal exams in spring 2023. By 2027, she hopes the Swedish supreme court will have delivered a verdict on Aurora's case.

'It's stressful because it's only three years before 2030, which has been given an unofficial deadline status for taking the measures necessary to keep global warming below 1.5 degrees.'

A district court in Nacka, bordering Stockholm, ruled in March 2023 that Aurora's case would be heard because it was 'legal enough', Edling says. 'By that they mean our case can be heard because it is not "political".'

A trial of this magnitude can appear prohibitively expensive. Aurora expect their case could cost 10 million Swedish Krona ($100,000). However, crowdfunding for cases of this type tends to be generous while legal advice is crowd-sourced through lessons learned in case law accrued in the Netherlands and elsewhere.

'There is an organisation called the Climate Litigation Network who offer invaluable help in formulating the law argumentation. The work has been done in it together, especially in Europe under the European convention on human rights, while I believe that there are similar collaborations in other regions. No one has to reinvent the wheel. There is knowledge in the community.'

200 cases of this nature have been brought to date, in every continent other than Antarctica.

'I live in the countryside and have seen the forests in Sweden's north chopped down in a very unsustainable manner. I live in a very privileged part of the world that has not seen before – and will not see for a while – the most drastic impacts of climate change or ecosystem deterioration.'

'Our activism is about two things. It's about inter-generational solidarity and equity, meaning that we need to make a future we can live in. And its about inter-generational equity, meaning that we need to make sure that it's possible to live in every place, especially the people who are least responsible for causing the climate crisis and are most affected.'

The top ten per cent of global emitters were responsible for nearly half of the total carbon dioxide emissions, research in 2019 from the United Nations Development Programme found.

'But it's also of course about protecting the environment that is close to us because it is inevitable that the ecosystems of the world are globally interlinked. So in order to protects the climate system we also need to protect our ecosystems, both globally and locally. That includes ecosystems in privileged places such as Sweden and perhaps particularly in Sweden because we have lots of forest. We log much of it and then we burn it up as bio-fuels.'

Edling is adamant that Aurora doesn't hold all the answers to respond to the emergency in time:

> The member base of our organisation overlaps with the member base of other youth climate organisations in Sweden. So we have members who are also part of the Friday strikes and also some that are involved in direct action. I think that is important – especially when we are talking about the timeline we are up against – because law can be a very powerful tool but it can also be a very slow tool.
>
> We need people to use other tools as well, in addition to the legal route. We need everyone to do what they can and to take their responsibility because I think that a diversified climate movement is a way more efficient one.

Thunberg is in agreement with Edling here and Sweden's 'original' youth climate activist is among those diversifying. In addition to backing Aurora's legal case, Thunberg embraced direct action in 2023. First she joined a coal protest in Germany. Then she linked up with Swedish direct action group Reclaim the Future, blocking the road for oil trucks in the port city of Malmo.

20-year-old Irma Kjellström is the woman behind Reclaim the Future, a tiny group which made global headlines after the Malmo action saw Thunberg arrested and face potential jail time. Thunberg ultimately escaped her first court hearing with a fine.

Kjellström joined Thunberg in court and I interviewed Kjellström the following day. I ask Kjellström whether Thunberg sees herself as a leader within the climate movement.

'I think maybe not,' Kjellström tells me, 'and if she does, it's as a sort of accidental leader. I think she's probably aware that she has a practical leadership role [but] something that has developed a lot within the youth climate movement is a very strong sense that we do things collectively.'

We've come to lean into and trust our experiences and feelings as young people, in this time of crisis, and as young people who have been born into a deadly system; young people who have been betrayed from the start really.

We've come to trust that and to speak really genuinely from that place, instead of trying to be anything else and trusting that saying exactly the things that we feel and think – as young people living through this – is best.

That's also the basis of the actions that we do. Those actions are also based on what it feels like to be a young person and to be in exactly the spot where a lot of your chances are being actively burned.

I can't really remember when I came to the realisation that a movement is needed for change to happen. Growing up in this time, it's always been in the background that things are not going well and everything is sort of threatened.

Kjellström tells me she was an early member of Extinction Rebellion (XR) Youth in Sweden and that it was through this membership that she first experimented with oil blockades:

It was when I saw movements grow and do things that it made me feel I could be part of it and I began growing into something concrete. And then through into Reclaim the Future, that grew out of an understanding of what was happening in the movement that already existed and what was needed. What was needed was for young people to take a bigger strategic hold of things and to create a new direction.

My first place in the climate movement was XR. For many, certainly not all, but many of us have been in XR or in the XR Youth section and done blockades there. A lot of our strategic thinking – or what we think is important or how we do things – is sort of taken from things that we've learned from XR or have come to think of through being in XR.

XR's big blockade in London in 2019 [the movement shut down every single road into central London] was one moment that has been really important – both when it happened and beyond it in the period since – because it has been channelled to get back to the feeling that things are possible: it's possible to mobilise; it's possible to make things happen; it's possible for things to quite suddenly change.

That moment has stuck in the imagination and memory of the climate movement. And in XR Sweden we also often return to that moment. It was in XR Youth in Sweden that we first decided that we were going to block a refinery, which was not something that XR had really done in Sweden before. We had no experience of doing anything like it and we just went for it and it went really, really well.

That was a very strengthening moment that has reassured us later of our direct action methods and in the feeling that even though we are young and don't have much experience, we can actually do quite a lot. That was an important moment internally that set the base for later things.

Direct action remains controversial, divisive and often illegal. However Kjellström says that national media coverage following Thunberg's appearance in court signalled a turning point in Swedish debate on the cause and tactics followed by some young climate activists.

'There was this article this morning in *Aftonbladet* [one of the highest circulating newspapers in Scandinavia]. It was the leader on the front, high up on their site, and the writer said that 'Greta is right' and 'doing these actions is exactly what is needed for change'. That's something that I never would have expected from that kind of writer in a big paper here.

A lot of the time we, as young activists, can feel very much like few people have our backs, that we won't be listened to when there are others with more life experience. But now there are powerful people in the media saying that we were right, basically.

Dr Elaine Daly, a lecturer at Blekinge Institute of Technology, has formed mixed opinions about the burgeoning activist spirit she has seen among students enrolling on the university's 'Strategic Leadership in Sustainability' masters programme in the five years since Thunberg first launched Fridays for Future:

The incoming knowledge of students is much higher than it was five years ago. I no longer need to go back to basics at the start. But now I have this challenge of: they think they know it all.

Our leadership programme really focuses on the individual's capacity and the inter-personal capacity, including the internal fortitude that you need as a change-maker to remain optimistic when faced with devastating statistics year on year about where our planet is going. How do you ensure you don't burn out? We work a lot with communities of practice, to ensure you're not an individual, but that you're one of many.

How do you restore your energy? How do you balance yourself? How do you achieve your own sustainability? We really look at the holistic view of what it takes to be a change-agent.

Thunberg has not studied Daly's course. Skipping school every Friday means it took until her 20th birthday before she graduated from secondary school.

Thunberg is indeed an 'accidental leader', rather than one shaped on any leadership degree course. However she has reinforced herself and her movement through finding her people, at Fridays for Future and at Aurora and at Reclaim The Future.

Each group is now borrowing from and strengthening one other.

'You need to find each other,' Aurora's Edling insists. 'You need to find a group of activists or engaged people who are willing to work very hard. The young people who are behind Aurora, we work free of charge and we put lots of time and energy into projects like this. Find each other and find a network that can support each other and work in a sustainable manner. Then the second thing is to find competence: find the scientists and lawyers and public relations people who can help you formulate an argument and use that platform to raise awareness of the climate crisis.'

I watch Thunberg quietly film and stream through her smartphone her activist friends from Kenya, advocating for Lake Victoria. I hear how she's leant on the leadership of Edling at Aurora and Kjellström at Reclaim the Future. I see a movement that is sustainably building its own future to win that of a generation.

CHAPTER THREE

FREETOWN CHRISTIANIA – A COMMUNE CLAIMING UNDERGROUND ENERGY

How do you win environmental arguments? Don't wait for permission, some say. The residents of Freetown Christiania didn't seek approval when they first established their commune in the former army barracks of Copenhagen, Denmark's capital city. Fifty years on, inhabitants reluctantly meet their new requirement to pay rent to the state, but the former squatters refuse to conform to the role of obedient tenants. Renewable energy systems, undetectable to their recently-appointed governmental landlords, are being quietly installed beneath the community's surrounding lakes.

'Often when you just do things, it is allowed,' says Kirsten Larsen, a social anthropologist. 'But when you *ask* to do things, it is not.' Responsible for the commune's 'press group', Larsen serves as a representative spokesperson for the community.

The septuagenarian has been living in Christiania since the days when the accommodation had no running water or electricity, but she retains the rebellious streak of the university students who first made the district their own.

Christianites have always pushed the boundaries. It started when they first occupied the living quarters left vacant by a modernising armed services half a century ago. 'Many more people came to Copenhagen to study in the '70s,' Larsen recalls.

'This squat came into being primarily because of a lack of housing. The army moved out because it was too old fashioned in here and then nobody wanted to take over. The state had a problem because they couldn't sell it... and then they just let us stay.'

Legally, the dynamic changed in 2012. A judge ruled that Christianites would have to pay rent to the state in order to continue to reside in the converted barracks, many of which are now brightly painted and homely, though some are still bereft of WCs and other hallmarks of conventional modern living.

'It was a very hard decision for us to receive. We had also run a case against the Danish state, to protect the public right to use, but we lost it. And when we lost it we had to decide whether to buy or rent. We decided to buy but the state only let us buy half of it. A conservative government had come in. They wanted to make money from us.'

Christianites were allowed to buy the commercial part of the district, a self-contained micro-economy that had developed through the formation of cafés, art galleries and the well-known 'pusher street', where the organised sale of cannabis, not harder drugs, is loosely tolerated by the Danish police.

'The old fortifications, which are under historical protection, we were not allowed to buy. We were forced to rent. We had to take loans to buy the city area. To finance things we took a guaranteed loan of something like 60 million Danish Krone [nine million Euros].'

The rent for the fortifications comes to around nine million Euros also (per year). These rents represent around a third of the average paid elsewhere in the city. However the experiences lived by Christianites in the 1970s compared with those endured through the courts in the decade just past have left a legacy seen in their prevailing mentality: victory is achieved through acting independently as a community, rather than through entrusting the apparatus of arbitration.

It explains their stealth choice and stealth application of a new renewable energy supply for the converted barracks: a geothermal system that captures heat from beneath the area's lakes – waterways that once provided a moat to protect the army.

Larsen does her best, in her second language, to do justice to the engineering that provides clean energy to heat her son's home, which is serving as the pilot for the wider community. 'You cannot see it because it's under the water,' she begins. 'It's a tube under the water, connected to a kind of well. They put it in and then it's connected to the house. So it's all underground and under the surface of the water. That's why you can't see it and why you can do it without the state getting involved.'

Ground-source heating is expensive to install, typically costing around 2,000 Euros. However its subterranean character offers promise for environmentally conscious tenants, with means, living beyond the tree-lined perimeters of Christiania's 900-person population.

The idea to experiment in Christiania was conceived by 'an organiser in the building office', who is unavailable for interview. 'I have a little bit of information from him but he is not very informative and there are reasons for that.' Kirsten continues. 'There was no permission from the state to make this installation and that's why he doesn't want to talk too much about it.'

'He had seen the technology used on visits to the Middle East and wanted to experiment. We want to make use of alternative energy and protect the world from carbon emissions.'

It's not the first time Christianites have demonstrated resourcefulness in bringing environmentally sustainable innovations to their community. 'It really started back in the year 2000. There had never been a water supply inside the houses before then and we only had electricity from 1990. It was not built for housing. It was cut-off. There were no installations....'

'So we took the chance to develop an alternative solution for the water problem. We used basins with a special kind of plant that can absorb the dirt from the waste water. It's a special kind of plant that they use also for fencing houses. We built nine of these basins in my area, where we are not connected to Copenhagen's sewage network. It's used for cleaning grey waste water from the bath and kitchen. We also have compost toilets.'

While Christianites refuse to seek permission from authorities for innovations they see as wholly benevolent, they are famous for their internal system of consensus democracy, where all neighbours are consulted on every proposal that is made. The method proved as inclusive and successful in this case as it has in other scenarios over the last 50 years.

'The heating system was turned on in October and the heat is good and sufficient. I think now when we build new houses, we will use it. It is quite expensive, which might hinder some people, but I think it will pay for itself over time.'

'In here, this kind of alternative solution is very popular. If it's possible to make it, almost everyone will say yes. We work with consensus, so if there is an overwhelming majority community feeling that that's what we want to do, then we'll do it.'

PART TWO

RACE WINS: INVERTING EDUCATION

CHAPTER FOUR
LESSONS FROM COLSTON – A STATUE'S NEW STATUS

Cleo Lake-Ayiih sought out an alternative education through 'activists from my own community: African-Caribbean,' after learning from her teachers 'absolutely nothing about the man Edward Colston was'.

Lake-Ayiih attended Colston Girls' School in Bristol, southwest England, in the 1990s. She remembers being walked down to the local cathedral on the first Friday of November each year to commemorate the slave-trader after whom her school was named. The ceremony by then attracted annual protests, attended largely by Black Bristolians. Lake-Ayiih, the daughter of an 'African father born in Jamaica' and a dual-heritage mother of Scots-Canadian lineage, heard their calls. Yet whenever she tried to raise the campaign with the school, she was 'immediately shut down'.

Later, upon being appointed mayor of the city, one of Lake-Ayiih's first acts was to remove from her new office a picture of Colston, photographed while he was executive director of the Royal African Company. Until recently widely revered in the city as a philanthropist, it has taken 200 years for Colston to be reviled by many for the fortune he made off the backs of enslaved Africans. Deference has been overtaken by defiance.

Lake-Ayiih established a Countering Colston movement that challenged the enduring physical legacy of the 'father of Bristol', calling for the removal of the merchant's name from concert halls and colleges. Most objectionable was the bronze statute standing, self-satisfied, in the city centre. 'It represented oppression, a complete denial and exclusion of a full detailed, inclusive history,' Lake-Ayiih says.

The statue was pulled down as part of peaceful and planned civil activism during Black Lives Matter protests in 2019, hurled into the harbour docks through which Colston's boats used to depart for Africa in the early 19th Century.

A survey commissioned by the We Are Bristol History Commission [a group formed in 2020 comprised of historians and researchers in the fields of law, art and culture, philosophy and trade unions] found strong support for the statue's removal across all demographics in Bristol except age, where there was a disparity. Helen McConnell-Simpson, a curator of social history at Bristol's M Shed museum, attributes this dividing line to a 'veneration of Edward Colston in schools in the earlier part of the 20th Century, where children were taught about his philanthropy and brought into the idea of him being one of the fathers of the city.'

McConnell-Simpson says it is her hope that the toppling of the statue can 'create a lasting shift in how we as a public think about, feel about and respond to racism' and believes museums, like curricula, have a decisive role to play in 'consolidating' change, through influencing older people, who in Bristol have been more reticent as a group, as well as the young.

'There's room for a really beneficial intergenerational conversation,' McConnell-Simpson continues, speaking at a time when the museum is assessing the most interactive way it can put the statue on permanent display. 'Personally I feel that museums should be radical organisations. It is important to welcome everybody and not only speak to a certain section of the population that hold particular views, that's obviously crucial, but I see museums as one of the last places where members of the public can come together and share views.'

'Politics and society have become so polarised and I think actually having more nuanced conversations is the thing that will move us forward in a progressive direction. Museums shouldn't be neutral, they should be holding space for really difficult conversations and they should challenge people to critique their views and listen to the views of others.

'However, that is quite a departure from what a lot of people have understood museums are for and it takes bravery from an organisational perspective to really embrace that. There are museums in the UK that do and I think they do it brilliantly, but there's also quite a strong political pressure not to take a more radical view and support that conversation. Museums are generally public bodies that need public funding and it's a difficult position to be in. Trying to find an ideological way through that is quite tricky.'

The installation of a digital display to sit alongside the statue at M Shed will maximise the number of voices that can contribute to ongoing conversations hosted at the museum about the enduring structural legacies of slavery.

Securing reparations for the communities of those whose families were trafficked across the Atlantic during the Colston era has been made a 'tangible' goal due to the role played by activists and creatives in accelerating a more widely shared understanding of British history, Lake-Ayiih believes. Reparations can now be realised 'quite quickly' following the toppling of the statue, she argues, pointing to the encouragement provided by 'loss and damage' compensation committed in 2022 to victims of the climate crisis.

'I think in terms of the mainstream having empathy, caring and even understanding this history, this British history, we have moved forward,' Lake-Ayiih says. 'The statue being pulled down was a landmark event and we are already seeing the impact of it. There were already a few actions on the boil, if you like, but those have definitely been sped-up now. The moment educated a lot of people, sparking them to find out more about the history.'

Bristol became the first city in the UK to pass a motion, raised by Lake-Ayiih during her time as Green Party mayor, recognising its complicity in the trans-Atlantic trafficking of enslaved Africans. Following the toppling of the statue, Lake-Ayiih says she has been approached directly by descendants of traffickers – individuals wanting to reconcile their family histories.

'Reparations is now a feasible topic that more people are talking about, whether that's here, or in America, or in the Caribbean. We are going to find people that are very, very wealthy – I've spoken to some of them – who have inherited wealth through enslavement. They are coming out and talking about it and wanting to see change, so I think there will be others who aren't responsible, but they've simply inherited some of this history, and this legacy, and some of the finance, and I think they will be looking to give something.'

'I think we can also question King Charles. Will he make a turn on things? Will he be the King who understands the Crown and the Royals' central role in this history?" Lake-Ayiih says Charles acknowledged a need for greater societal understanding of enslavement during a visit to an exhibitition of Black British History in Leeds staged by The World Reimagined – a national education art project transforming how the transatlantic slave trade's enduring impact is understood – shortly after succeeding the Queen as monarch. She says:

> I feel we are not far away now from the racial justice we want to see. The toppling of the statue continues to be spoken about and I think it will still be of massive significance in years if not generations to come.

> There will always be some negativity about the way it came down but the argument of waiting for permission or endorsement from the powers-that-be kind of sends society back to the structures that necessitated change in the first place. Politics can never truly reflect society and collective action will always be more human, bring on board people who don't vote, and more accurately reflect the true consensus in existence during any moment in time.

> Reparations shouldn't be framed as something that either the government or taxpayer should pay. The taxpayer was paying back the debt paid to slave-owners until 2015, it turns out. Rather, let's step up the tracking and tracing of the compensation and wealth from enslavers' plantation owners to see where that is today. The redress should come from people who directly inherited a lot of wealth and still have a lot of that wealth. That can be institutional, that can be families, but it is important to recognise that many of the politicians of that day and also many of the mayors of

that period were also heavily invested in enslavement. This is about restoration, about equity.

The Colston Girls' School Lake-Ayiih attended was renamed Montpelier High as one of many outcomes of the Countering Colston campaign she initiated, with her own legacy now eclipsing that of the man Lake-Ayiih defined herself against. Invited by teachers to make a recent return to a former classroom, the activist met and mentored students, including one group who have set themselves up to scrutinise the diversity of curricula being followed by schools across the region.

'It's a very different school to the one I attended. It's become a breeding ground for socially engaged young people.'

CHAPTER FIVE
BLACK LIVES MATTER – POLICE PUSHED OUT OF SCHOOLS

❨The last part of the 20ᵗʰ Century and start of the 21ˢᵗ Century silenced us with false promises that if we just shut the fuck up and did what we were told, maybe we'd be Oprah or Puffy or LeBron, or, dare we say it, Barack Obama,' writes Patrisse Khan-Cullors, one of the three founding members of Black Lives Matter, in her memoir *When They Call You a Terrorist*.

'The truth is that the overwhelming majority of us spent a good portion of our time battling white supremacy, whether we knew it or not.'

Khan-Cullors describes the 'American Movement *Against* Black Lives' that manifests in August 2014. A stand-off between the Black community of Ferguson, a small town of 21,000 residents, and the police has ensued after unarmed 18-year-old Mike Brown dies after being shot in the head, chest and hands by a white police officer. The victim is the same age, height and weight as Khan-Cullors' brother Monte, a survivor of police torture. She identifies profoundly with the victim's family.

One of the first pictures that emerges of the protests features a Black girl holding a sign bearing the message Black Lives Matter. She is standing in front of a vehicle that has reasonably been described as a tank. The mine-resistant armoured truck was first deployed by the US military, designed specifically for use in the Iraq war, before being taken up by police.

The military equipment used in the response to the protests, Khan-Cullors writes, has been financed through legalised police extortion' of the Black community.

Asset forfeiture, which had grown to become a 'three-billion dollar industry' at the time of Brown's killing enabled police to seize property if they suspected someone of being involved in the drugs trade, with or without proof. Equipment such as the tanks deployed in Ferguson were purchased from revenue generated by asset seizures of this kind.

As has been well documented, smartphone reels of police brutality put some power back in the hands of a community routinely terrorised by law enforcement. 'Moments videoed by bystanders animated our pain and rage and resolve,' Khan-Cullors summarises.

But Black Lives Matter is a story that pre-dates smartphones and the infamous recording of the last breaths of Black men killed by police, most notoriously George Floyd, for whose murder a white officer was eventually convicted.

'Living in patriarchy means the default is to de-centre the role of women and their work," reflects Khan-Cullors, who founded Black Lives Matter alongside fellow artist-activists Alicia Garza and Opal Tometi.

With all three having recently retired from front-line leadership of the movement, I turn to BLM's new leader, Cicley

Gay, to learn more about the energy, tactics and social impacts already delivered by what has always been a largely women-led movement.

'Thank you for asking me about my "why" Gay says softly. 'I am the mother of three black sons. I rarely say that I am a single mother – though I am – because there is nothing singular about the community of support that has held me and my three sons over the course of the past 20-plus years.'

> I am in this position for every single mother who holds their chest in their breath in hope and prayer when one of their Black children leaves the house every day... in fear of the call that they received that they are not coming home.

> I was moved when Trayvon Martin was killed eleven years ago. We're celebrating obviously the tenth year of Black Lives Matter. I saw Trayvon [an unarmed Black teenager from Florida who was killed while returning home from a trip to the shops to buy Skittles sweets for this brother] in my three sons.

> I recognise that I have a commitment to give back to the community that's given so much to me. And so when I think about my 'why', it's absolutely my three sons, and the work that I've done in investing in them and *preparing them for the world*. I say too that it's now my responsibility to also *prepare the world for them*.

> We're evolving as a foundation. In 2020, when things became more public and there was the largest protest of people shouting Black Lives Matter across the world and they took to the streets, there were a lot of people and

organisations who believed that we solely existed for the continuation of those protests.

While we absolutely believe that there is a place for protest and there absolutely is a place to keep the pressure on, the foundation in of itself is about the fullness of Black life. While [protest] is a part of it we know that there's a lot more to do in other areas in addition to the protest work, the grass roots frontline work.

Black people are very full, whole human beings and we want to inject resources into all the areas of their life, as opposed to us being reactive as it relates to a tragedy occurring in one of our communities.

Black Lives Matter received some 90 million dollars from donors in 2020 and under Gay's leadership as chair, it has begun putting that money into changing Black lives through six specific areas of work.

'We are organising resources into building Black social, economic and political power. We are strategically doing that through investing in six areas:

- grass roots action
- healing justice
- policy
- research
- arts
- culture

'We often say that we're accountable when we're specific and so we carved out those six ways to dig deeper and ensure that people understand that we're making substantive change to reach Black people and Black communities holistically.

'We are not a for-profit business and so we are not necessarily thinking about a return on those investments financially. But we are demonstrating impact in many of those ways which will hopefully encourage folks to continue to give. And that's not just individuals, who continue to support us. It's also corporations that we're holding accountable and other larger foundations as well.'

Black Lives Matter continues to bring in nine million dollars a year and it describes itself as the largest philanthropic, abolitionist organisation that's ever existed.

'When we say "abolitionist", we mean just that: that we are dismantling structures of policing and violence in our community. To disrupt that system means that we've got to disrupt philanthropy too and we challenge ourselves to do that every day.'

Gay takes pride in the fact that the very saying 'Black Lives Matter' has belatedly become a normalised 'position', a rallying cry 'amplified by a sitting US president via his state of the union address and social media accounts'. When Obama left office, America had the smallest federal prison population in a generation, a direction of travel aligned with the modern abolitionist path advocated for by Black Lives Matter.

Moreover, Gay points to the 'demilitarisation' of education systems as another landmark success story of the movement:

> We've made great strides in creating cultures of care, reducing violence in schools and even sometimes reducing contracts with police organisations who are not necessarily there to protect but to inflict more damage and more harm in our communities.

We've had lots of success in terms of people recognising that Black lives do matter. But we've got a lot of work to do because it's a fight at every turn, particularly when we make progress.

There are schools and colleges that have actually ended their contracts with local police departments and they are working to phase a police presence out of their campuses in favour of mental health and social staff. Those schools are in places including Seattle, Washington, Oakham in California and Minneapolis in Minnesota – which has been in the news so much because of the violence perpetrated there and in Milwaukee.

It was in Minneapolis that George Floyd was murdered by police officer Derek Chauvin, making the policy legacy in schools here particularly profound.

'We're looking not only at what folks need in terms of physical safety, but also emotional and financial safety. The Black Lives Matter Global Network Foundation stepped in, for example, when legislators in the United States failed to pass student debt relief. So many students are grappling with this debt, including millions of Black people.'

Gay reveals she figures among those still burdened by student loan repayments. 'We're creating what we call a student solidarity fund. While we may not be directly addressing necessarily the one-to-one violence that's happening within schools, we are challenging the policing and police presence, to create new systems of care and think holistically about how we support students at every single level, from elementary school to college.'

I ask how the scaling back of policing in schools has been achieved, whether it was through protest, activism, diplomacy or something else. She says:

It's been a combination of all (of the above). We looked at following the money and there is actually a current initiative in California called Cancel the Contract. Myself and others at Black Lives Matter looked at the re-direction of financial resources and demonstrated that if we look at where the budgets lie and where the money is going, the return-on-investment around investing in young people as opposed to increasing police presence would result in less police time. This is because when people need mental health support, that can be an indicator of more violent behaviour.

We also realised that police in schools were often the perpetrators of violence and we had to prove that through advocacy, through activism, through research. We also had to keep the pressure on in terms of forcing local legislators to listen to their constituents and to provide to them what they needed and what their children needed.

We've made some gains in those communities and it makes it a lot easier in other communities when we can demonstrate success. It's been a multi-faceted approach. It's been advocacy; it's been activism; it's been paying attention to budgets. Our impact on creating a culture of care in schools has come also from creating a groundswell of support – amongst the people who are often the ones in a position to be victimised by police – for change to be made.

As in the UK, a legacy of the anti-racist movement that was catalysed in 2020 following the death of George Floyd has been the diversification of teaching materials within schools. However this has faced greater resistance in the US.

There are systems and institutions here that have made substantive changes. School administrators in cities like Denver, Colorado, and Spokane, Washington, have updated their curricula to include more diverse authors, historians and subjects. And they are delivering specific anti-racist teaching.

It is one of our biggest fights right now, because a lot of the time, the language around adapting curricula has been manipulated. People are thinking that we're teaching folks to be victims, or teaching others that they are responsible for the dehumanising of black people, when the reality is that we just want folks to know the truth, right?

What we have found is that the school districts who are adopting racial equity policies are sometime desegregating schools: they're closing the racial gaps amongst students and reforming the way they teach and even discipline students.

A lot of that starts with the hiring of staff and thinking about who is actually on board in terms of their staff make-up and who is generally invested in shifting the culture within school systems.

We're also talking at a very high level with many donors who fund educational institutions and educational structures. Increasingly now they are requiring grantees – the folks who receive the funding – to implement diversity, equity and inclusion policies, or at least speak to them before they receive the funding.

It may not be that people are completely on board holistically. But if you've got some funding attached to anti-racist change then it may at least make them think twice about how they activate their policies or how they run their programmes within school systems.

Black Lives Matter is now on billboards and on artists' murals all over the country and if you think about the media and arts, it's a part of who we are as a country now and as a world.

I also think about the backlash that we've received. Over the course of time, throughout history, one of the ways to actually demonstrate or indicate whether or not we're being successful is often to look at where people who are against our movement and our work are most angry. In the United States now, that's education. We've got critical race theory; we've got affirmative action. Those are the things now that are being shifted and attacked by antagonists.

After the life of George Floyd was stolen we started doing the work to build a foundation that would exist to continue to pour resources into the community. We did this so that we can be here for the long-term, until the work is done.

A 2017 Pew study found that 54 per cent of white people viewed officer-involved shootings involving Black people to be signs of a broader problem. This attitudinal shift created a policy window for local, state, and federal changes to policing and the criminal justice system.

Black Lives Matter sparked a series of policy and organisational changes to policing that include implicit bias trainings, body-worn cameras [though these are still often turned off], and bans on 'no-knock' arrest warrants.

'We're intervening on existing and new policies to reimagine a world without punitive measures. So if we believe that people imagined a world with policing and jails, we believe that people can imagine another way.

'We're thinking about a world where Black people can have all of the things they need: food, education, housing, healthcare, water, breathable air, everything that is foundational to community safety.'

PART THREE

BIRTH RIGHTS: HUMAN STORIES

CHAPTER SIX
ABORTION ABOUT-TURN – CONSTITUTION REPEALED

'Abortion doctors want to stay on-side with our president,' a Turkish social worker told me, after walking me silently up to her office on the fourth floor of a women's shelter in Istanbul. Recep Tayyip Erdoğan has chilled reproductive rights in the nation he has ruled since 2013.

'Abortion is murder,' Erdoğan told a women's conference in 2012. 'One or two children mean bankruptcy,' he insisted a year later, warning Turkey's economy was at risk of an ageing population. 'Three children means we are not improving but not receding either. So, I repeat, at least three children are necessary in each family.'

How did women respond? 'We asked him, "Who is going to look after these children? Are you going to do it?"' recalls Gulsan Kanat-Dinc, a social worker at the Purple Roof women's shelter in Istanbul, Turkey's largest city. Childcare provision for under-threes does not exist here. To no-one's great surprise, families did not begin creating larger families in order to bolster an already booming economy.

A fertility study published by the *Lancet* journal in the year we speak, 2018, found Turkey's 'net reproductive rate' actually fell in the intervening years, in line with a global trend, dropping to just 0.8. While natives of child-rearing age had 1.8 children, their counterparts in Egypt averaged 2.7 offspring.

Meanwhile, the Turkish economy was finally faltering after a long period of buoyancy. Inflation reached 25 per cent in October 2018.

Disturbingly, while the law has not changed, hospital responses to abortion requests in Istanbul have. There has been a radical shift in order to meet Erdoğan's public advocacy and expectations.

'We are seeing more victims of domestic rape contact us than ever before, saying they are unable to find a hospital that will provide them a free abortion,' says Kanat-Dinc. Purple Roof does not tally calls of this nature but the social worker estimated receiving as many as 100 such calls in a 12- month period. 'I think the state hospitals want to show that they are with him [Erdoğan]. In Istanbul there are still a few hospitals that provide free abortions, but there are less and less.'

The organisation supports Istanbulis to find the few remaining public hospitals that still perform 'no-questions asked' abortions. 2013 research from Istanbul's Kadir Has University found that eight per cent of state hospitals provide abortion services no-questions-asked, which is permitted by the current law, while 78 percent provide abortions only when there is a medical necessity for it. A 2020 follow-up survey from Kadir Has found that all state hospitals had ceased providing the service.

'We do public opinion surveys annually and what we've seen is public support for women's right to abortion is eroding,' says Professor Mary Lou O'Hara, Director of Women and Gender Studies at Kadir Has. 'When we ask people whether they agree with the question Do you think abortion is a sin?" or "Do you think it's the sacrifice of an innocent life?" those figures have gone up every year since we started collecting the data in 2013.'

The pattern correlates with Erdoğan first making his outspoken abortion polemics. It also coincides with a crackdown on all opposing viewpoints since the 'Gezi protests' in 2013. What started as an environmental protest at Gezi Park in central Istanbul morphed into a weeks-long civil rights uprising. The United Nations has reported that around 200,000 'opponents of the government', have faced detention since then, sometimes for months or years without charge.

All public institutions have faced purges, including hospitals. The period of oppression has even seen doctors face six-figure fines for treating patients injured as activists. A two year state-of-emergency granting the government special powers to bypass human rights law has at least now been lifted.

However, a constitutional referendum that took place during that period granted Erdoğan ongoing powers to govern by decree and the opportunity to potentially rule until 2034. He was re-elected once again in 2023, confounding some polling forecasts. A culture of fear and submission to state desires has permeated, extending to doctors qualified to perform abortions.

'The vast majority of doctors and patients are at public hospitals and you have an entire computer system which tracks these things,' explains O'Hara. 'All procedures are recorded in a system centralised in the health ministry. . It's a system of incentive and disincentive: it's how doctors are evaluated.'

Each procedure has a certain amount of points. Things related to reproductive health have a very low amount of points. So there's not a lot of incentive to build points, earn promotion or earn extra pay in the system; to be engaged in reproductive health work inside the system.

It's just not worth doing abortions. If you operate in an environment where you sense that it will be frowned upon, whether it is or not, you'll regulate yourself, you'll put more of your energy or emphasis in this area or that area because then you won't get into trouble.

It's the kind of thing that doesn't usually get into the paper but stories come to me about people who are treated badly in seeking an abortion. They've been humiliated, not treated very kindly.

A system of institutional discrimination has built up, without any changes to abortion law itself.

Women who had not found a sympathetic hospital, or who had not yet been reached by Purple Roof, faced private clinic fees of between 1,200 and 4,500 Turkish Lira (£200-£700) when these fees were sourced in 2018. This was before the jump in inflation, after which prices spiked again, along with the cost of the morning-after pill and imported contraception too.

Fewer than half of Turkish female adults are in employment and there are long waiting lists for scant childcare options. The cost of a private abortion is more than a month's salary for those on the minimum wage.

'On one hand it's amazing that abortion's legal, it's not an election issue and is potentially free,' O'Hara said. 'Yet in Tukey you cannot attain your rights if you don't have the money. Horrible. The [desired] environment is when women can make these choices for themselves, when it's not the social environment, or the political environment or the economic environment making the choice for them.'

While access to reproductive rights was shutting down in Turkey in 2018, the opposite was unfolding in Ireland, following a remarkable referendum victory won by pro-choice activists.

The Abortion Rights Campaign (ARC) is a grass roots all-volunteer group dedicated to achieving free, safe and legal abortion care everywhere on the island of Ireland, for everyone who wants or needs it. ARC was one of the three core groups that formed the civil society organisation Together for Yes, which successfully campaigned for a 'yes' vote in the referendum to repeal the eighth amendment from the Irish constitution in May 2018.

Richael Carroll, National Convenor at ARC, described to me three decisive factors that saw their campaign secure 66.4 per cent of the vote. The first 'key' was that the island was experiencing renewed belief that constitutions can be amended, with Marriage Equality recently having been introduced for the LGB community. Second was raising awareness of the vulnerability and injustice attached to the eighth amendment. Third was the impact made on the public and in turn politicians, once the issue was humanised through the death of Savita Halappanavar, a pregnant dentist of Indian heritage neglected by doctors under the prevailing terms of the constitution.

Savita's family said she asked several times for her pregnancy to be terminated because she had severe back pain and was miscarrying. Her husband said doctors refused because there was a foetal heartbeat. Savita later died of septicaemia.

Staff at University Hospital Galway had told the family Ireland was 'a Catholic country'. Investigators concluded Savita died by 'medical misadventure' and recommended changes to the legal situation.

'I was involved in the marriage equality movement in 2015 and when the yes vote won, that's when I realised that with our legislative system you could actually change things, believe it or not, if you put energy towards it,' Carroll recalls.

> So many people that were involved with Marriage Equality jumped across into the Repeal campaign because we saw that grassroots movements spread out to local communities could actually affect real change. The people that voted in the Marriage Equality referendum, once they saw that you could actually make things happen, then they wanted to get involved in a political movement for what was the first time for many. It was quite wonderful and felt miraculous to many. It was nothing new to me because I'd been involved in a lot of other things, but it was new to a lot of other people.

> I was speaking to someone, a friend who got in contact, and they told me about another cause that I would be interested in, around the eighth amendment. At the first meeting I went to I was very disorganised. But when I heard there that the eighth amendment stops women from having consent during pregnancy, that's when I said: 'sign me up!' That was enough for me to know that I needed to be involved in making this thing 'go away'.

When Savita died, it kind of went over my head a bit that it was because of the eighth amendment that she lost her life. Maybe it wasn't pushed enough at the time that that's why she died, or maybe I lost that part of the story. But once I realised how bad the eighth amendment was, how restrictive it was, how much suffering it was causing, there was no way I couldn't be involved.

I have asked myself why it [the cause] got me. The idea that in your most vulnerable hour, your right to consent to things was taken away from you, was just not right to me. You should have a right to choose with everything about safety when pregnant, whether it's a home birth, whether it's an epidural... it should be about making it safe for people. It makes me so cross just thinking about it, even after it's gone...!

Pregnant women have been dying in Ireland for years, but in religious nations, this fact often becomes secondary. 'I think it was hearing people's stories,' Carroll reflects. 'It's a terrible thing to have to be needed. It's not just people "wanting" to have abortions. It's people being genuinely so heartbroken about not being able to bring their babies into the world, then experiencing terrible, desperate abandonment in the weeks leading up to the birth, who have died with their baby in the womb."

This reality radicalised and united people to get involved. Once the eighth amendment was shown in that way, and that change is possible, you can't allow that to happen. People had been left to die for hundreds of years. For it to still be happening by 2018... it was just beyond belief.

The more referendum opinion polls that came out, the more politicians who were vocal on the 'no' side came out and flipped to saying, 'Oh yes, it's a great idea'. It was similar to when Irish prime minister Leo Varadkar had said that gay people shouldn't be allowed to adopt children, on the record, and then went on to say the opposite.

For someone to come into our country, as Savita had, and for us to treat them so badly, was hugely embarrassing for people in Ireland. A successful, wonderful woman, trying to make her life for herself in this country – and she was ignored, not listened to – and there have been a few cases like this since of people of colour treated very similarly. There were quite a few younger people like Savita before, but I think because there wasn't a face to these people, they didn't grab people's attention.

We had first her husband talking, then her community. People couldn't ignore that. It was a real person's story. It was very clear why this legislation needed to change. We had ignored someone who was dying, who was going into septic shock and they just let her die, they didn't do anything. You can't have doctors not doing anything and the eighth amendment was the only reason why she died.

The wording of the referendum question that was ultimately put to the public on legalising abortion was framed by a citizens' assembly, a group of 99 individuals representing the diversity of the nation.

The members were chosen at random to reflect the Irish population in terms of age, gender, social class and geography. They included pro-lifers, pro-choicers and undecideds.

Together they deliberated on abortion across five weekends, over five months between November 2016 and April 2017. The assembly heard from people from both sides of the abortion debate, including medical, legal and ethical specialists, and people giving personal testimonies about their experiences. Members were also given the opportunity to discuss amongst themselves and to consider the views of others in the room.

Ultimately, the assembly recommended a referendum and shaped the wording of the question. The ratio of 'yes' to 'no' votes in the referendum mirrored almost exactly the split in the assembly itself, reflecting the quality of the membership selection and verification process.

An *Irish Times*/Ipsos MRBI poll in May 2017 indicated that just 23 per cent of the public were in favour of legalising abortion in all circumstances. However, once the public had had a chance to consider the matter more deeply during the referendum campaign, a new reality emerged.

In the assembly 64 per cent voted in favour of 'terminations without restrictions'. In the referendum, 66 per cent voted in favour of repealing the eighth amendment, effectively legalising abortion in the Republic of Ireland.

A citizens' assembly had been tried and tested previously in Ireland, when the country deliberated on same-sex marriage. This format of citizen-led participative democracy has since been advocated for by groups pulling for other causes, such as Extinction Rebellion through their environmental demands, described in the first chapter of this book.

Campaigning for 'yes' in Ireland was largely co-ordinated remotely, through WhatsApp and video calls. Initially Carroll worked as convenor for the Mayo region, and only one in-person meeting was staged in the county, away from annual marches.

'Having a physical presence together at the marches was important for the media, but also for solidarity, to give each other a hug... and, at our celebratory march in 2018, to say "Well done".'

CHAPTER SEVEN
ZIKA SURVIVORS – BIO-IDENTITIES AVOIDED IN BRAZIL

In 2016, having recently become a parent for the first time, I travelled to Brazil. The country was grappling with the 'Zika crisis'. The mosquito-induced health emergency saw thousands of babies born with microcephaly, a disabling health condition.

I visited Pestalozzi, an organisation that provides social care and education, based in the north of Rio de Janeiro state. The nurses were supporting nine very young children born with microcephaly. Five of these, those impacted by the most severe symptoms, were living with microcephaly known to be caused by the Zika virus.

One member of staff used his finger and thumb to make a shape an inch wide to illustrate the head-size of new-borns that had been brought to them. It was an upsetting visit and I came away rooting for Pestalozzi, but uncertain as to how much they could do for children, knowing many more parents would come to them for support in the weeks and months ahead.

I was aware of children that had been born with microcephaly in the past going on to surpass the limited expectations others had of them. The respected journalist Ann Carolina Caseres, a Brazil native, represented a symbol of hope.

However I was also acutely aware from family experiences of my own that conditions manifesting in brain seizures need sophisticated neurological and nursing expertise and carefully managed medicinal experimentation.

I inquired whether the Brazilian government was providing any extra money for Pestalozzi to source the specialist health care professionals require to treat children presenting the most complex needs the organisation had faced in its 69-year-history.

The answer was 'no'. A £5 contribution towards therapy sessions to aid with motor/mobility development was the only support the state was providing. This partial subsidy had been flat for a decade and remained so at the outset of the Zika crisis. The country's economy was struggling, with debt at both national and state level rising.

It was a poignant visit to Pestalozzi, made on my first trip outside the country since our own baby was born. I was struck also by the juxtaposition of the state neglect facing thousands of disabled children, set against the backdrop of Rio de Janeiro hosting the first Paralympic Games to come to South America. A gloriously vibrant carnival was laid on for the opening ceremony. Would the children's lives be filled with any colour of their own as they grew up?

In 2023 I established a connection with a medical anthropologist based in Recife in north-eastern Brazil, the epicentre of the Zika crisis. I wanted to hear how events were playing out for Brazil's 'Zika Babies', who had now reached school age. My own seven-year-old daughter entertained herself in our living room while I commenced a lengthy video call with Dr Parry Scott, a gentle and time-generous Professor of Anthropology at the Federal University of Pernambuco.

I kept the door to the living room shut and wore headphones, for I was not expecting an uplifting conversation. The majority (59 per cent) of disabled people in Brazil live in institutions rather than the community for at least six years of their lives, while the charity Minority Rights Group (MRG) has documented the double discrimination faced by disabled people of colour in Brazil, with high ratios of this demographic in and around Recife.

Evidence from MRG and Human Rights Watch suggests that Black people with disabilities are more likely to be incarcerated and denied their human rights and fundamental freedoms than white people with disabilities. People with disabilities are more likely to be placed under state care in institutions, where violations of rights regularly occur including restraining, guardianship (deprivation of legal capacity), medication without consent, and lack of access to education.

According to the Ministry of Health, 84 per cent of the mothers of children with Congenital Zika Syndrome are Black and around two-thirds of these mothers are located in the northeast of Brazil. The vast majority are also young (71 per cent between 15 and 29 years old); and many are single, separated or widowed (49 per cent).

While I am fearing the worst, Professor Scott is quick to tell me of how organisation achieved through associations, led predominantly by Black Brazilian mothers, has enabled children living with Zika to access not just a better quality of life than may have been anticipated, but stigma itself has also been mitigated.

Associations lobbied diligently and successfully, Professor Scott tells me, to secure access to life-long welfare support, medical and social support, and primary education, largely non-residential.

The associations were an extremely important mediator between the health systems, the health professionals and the families. The two most active associations were extraordinarily important both in giving voice and in helping the health system to understand what they had to do to help the children. The associations amplified mothers' ideas of what should be looked into in terms of health, ensuring these ideas were better known.

AMA – the Alliance of Mothers and Families of Children with Rare Diseases – deals with care for the children and for care givers. The other association is called UMA – the Union of Mothers of Angels. The idea that has been expressed is that these children are angels and the mothers of angels are going to [navigate] with these children who are born with a problem.

The experience for mothers could have been one of absolute suffering, not knowing how to navigate a health system their children were born into. The associations provide guides, legal advice, advice on how to approach mental health support and meetings of reinforcement.

I ask Professor Scott what he means by 'meetings of reinforcement'. 'Spaces to generate a collective feeling of "we're all in this together; there's a citizenship level to this experience where we have a right to be treated as well as possible and a responsibility to be very clear about what we need".'

The associations were the ones who really got to know the families, the names of the mothers and children and their brothers and sisters. The associations inserted their administrators responsible for the care of children with learning disabilities, gastrointestinal needs and so on into the meetings with the state.

These meetings involving the associations and the state – in our case Pernambuco state – were tense meetings. The state was trying to show it was doing all it could to help people but they came to recognise they could lean on the associations to make sure everybody – or at least as many people as possible – were reached when there were donations or when there were new ways of treating things. The associations became a vehicle for understanding what was going on, and for families to make their demands known.

Ultimately, a synergy was found between the mediator role played by the associations and a 'national and state pride that was triggered by the need to respond to what the World Health Organisation went on to declare a global health emergency.'

Liberia, Guinea and Sierra Leone, when they were dealing with Ebola, they didn't know how to do things all by themselves and they had to have help from people from the outside.

From Recife to Sao Paulo, there was a determination that 'we're going to respond better than when the countries impacted by Ebola had to respond to that disease. If we have international support then that's good but it's not going to be the case that we're going to depend on other countries to answer this question. We're going to do it ourselves and show that we're good at it.'

The researchers were very anxious to turn out strong and professional research. The health system said, 'we're able to restructure ourselves, re-organise ourselves enough so that there will be rehabilitation centres; places where physiotherapy can be done. We'll also make sure that the kinds of special needs that the children have in terms of gastro-intestinal problems and all the other diverse symptoms are responded to through our building of good systems'.

Since Zika was concentrated here, there was a sense that it was 'our' disease. The importance of dealing with the disease became a matter of national pride and local pride. Inter-relations between states in Brazil are such that they have a kind of competition that can be healthy for responding to emergencies of this kind.

The hardest challenge for the families was battling a sense that the readiness with which they shared information with researchers was not matched by the accessibility with which they could receive it back in return. There were complaints that computerised systems should have been made more intuitive, empowering patients to more easily reach the health information collected about their child in order to share it with the next specialist who needed it.

Professor Scott says he empathises with the parents. He outlived his own disabled son, who died one year before we speak. However he points out that an increasing number of the mothers of children born with Zika no longer recognise any medical needs within their children, a triumphant legacy of the work done by the associations and the health systems in Brazil in delivering effective rehabilitative treatments and therapy.

The mothers will say, 'he has a syndrome, but he's not sick. He's fine. He's in good health now. He *had* problems.' So it's a question now of continuing to make people understand that the children are not just 'people who go to the health system'.

In Brazil, we don't hear people say 'this is a Zika child.' People are very aware of Zika because it was very important here, but it's not going to become a 'bio-identity' for the children in the way that we have seen in the past with children who have leukaemia, for example.

Ironically, the success of unravelling the risk of becoming associated primarily with a bio-identity appears largely down to bio-identity associations. But it's to the benefit of the children of the mothers who led those associations (associations that are becoming less politically activity now they no longer need to be).

'These children now are eight years old and they're going around trying to be another kid in the family and letting everyone understand that. The new demands now entail living in day-to-day situations within a system that has sensitivity to their needs and I think that's what our work is – to make sure that that sensitivity continues to be available.'

PART FOUR

HEALTH AND HEALING: CREATIVE CONFRONTATION

CHAPTER EIGHT
POLITICIANS PERSUADED –
MEDICAL CANNABIS LEGALISED

'Fifty years of government failure.' That's how critics characterise the lack of progress since UK legislators passed the Misuse of Drugs Act, way back in 1971. 'Yeah, but it's fifty years of failure from us [reformists] as well,' continues Paul North, Director of Volteface. The London-based organisation he runs has grown to become one of the world's most creative pressure groups, seeking to reduce the harm drugs pose to individuals and society through evidence-based policy reform.

'I don't think we've done an amazing job,' North insists. 'Criminalisation is going up, drug-related deaths are going up every year.'

I ask North what motivated him to join Volteface as a policy officer in 2016. 'My background is in criminology. I studied criminology at university. I ended up working in drug treatment services. I worked my way up from harm reduction to managing teams treating complex drug addiction. I did that for nine years.

It's fucking hard work; really taxing. And then I just needed to do something else.'

'I saw the harm that drug policy was having on vulnerable people and I thought I'd really like to try and change things at sort of a higher level.'

What change did you want to see?

> I just wanted to see more compassion really. Less criminal-isation. Not compassion without consequence – I'm not by any means of the view that there aren't criminal activities. Or that drugs are harmless. But I wanted to see adequate funding for people with a problem and less arrests of people made for possession of drugs.

> I was really frustrated by the devastation that I saw that a single offence can have. The single possession of a drug that is used by millions of people. How significant that can be to someone's life. I've never been of the view that we should legalise everything. Cannabis is very different to cocaine.

Upon trading work on the frontline for a role geared towards affecting policy change, North's frustration initially only grew. 'I would fly politicians to Canada and show them its decriminalised approach to drugs. They would be like, "This is great, I support this now." But then we would fly back to England and I would speak with them again when they were around senior politicians and they would say, "I can't support this."'

> If you try to engage politicians with such a moral issue as drugs, then they become obsessed with, 'What are people going to say?' They don't say, 'What's good for the people?'

They say, 'What will people think?' And that's modern politics. That's how the political establishment operate, they all do it. The first thing they ask is, 'What will the people think?'

Once you accept that, then what is the point in engaging with them on a subject that's complicated? It's a total waste of time. Because of that, the best thing to do is to move the things that are around them, to educate the public, so that their support reduces the fear of the political establishment.

Reconciled to reality, Volteface flipped their approach on its head. The next person they would fly to Canada would not be a British politician. It would be the British mother of a child whose epilepsy could only be contained by a cannabis-based treatment, one that could be purchased legally only on the other side of the Atlantic.

Charlotte Caldwell, mother of Billy Caldwell, had been encouraged by a friend to contact Volteface. Billy was experiencing dozens of seizures daily at the time and Charlotte was committed to doing anything that would get the treatment that would save her son. North recalls:

We flew Charlotte to Canada to get a legal cannabis prescription – I mean legal in Canada – and it reduced his seizures from 100 a day to zero: incredible. We then flew her back to London Heathrow with cannabis oil and we got her to say at Customs: 'I've got cannabis oil in my bag and it was prescribed by a doctor and it's reduced my son's seizures by 100 a day.'

Customs obviously took the cannabis oil off her and said 'That's a class B drug, that's not allowed.' Then we had a press conference on the other side of the gate with all the main news there and it just caused absolute chaos for the government. It put them under so much pressure.

They took the medication off her. He started having seizures again. They took him to hospital. It was Theresa May in power at the time, who's probably the most conservative prime minister we've had in Britain. She then became like, 'We're going to have to legalise this for medical use.'

But it wasn't due to government engagement. It wasn't due to the government suddenly caring about the issue. At all. They couldn't give a shit. It was down to the public going, 'Why can't you give the kid his medication? It's horrendous.' It was that that drove it through and got it – suddenly, out of nowhere – tabled in parliament and passed as legislation without any resistance from the House.

We'd looked around the world and saw that that those campaigns worked and knew it would be successful. Because drug use is such a moral issue the only way you create widespread support is to bypass the morality, or play into the morality.

In America, *Charlotte's Web*, a CNN documentary broadcast five years earlier, had drawn attention to medical marijuana treating seizures previously endured by a five-year-old girl living with Dravet syndrome. The case is credited with changing attitudes and laws in the States.

North had studied *Charlotte's Web* along with the work of Jonathan Haidt, a psychologist who has authored books on what united social conservatives and liberals. 'You learn that the thing that everyone will support is stopping kids getting hurt. No-one's going to say, "The kid's going to die of epilepsy." Everybody's going to say, "Give the kid the fucking medicine."

> The only way to get Billy the medicine was to re-schedule the drug [re-classify it as legal for medical use]. The government really had no choice. And this is I why believe that the less government engagement the better because they're going to do what they're going to do and they don't act in the interests of the people; they act in the interest of the votes, on both sides of the House. Labour are just as bad as the Tories. They're horrendous. Politicians just think, 'What do I do to stay popular?' rather than 'What do I do for the interests of the people?'

> With medical cannabis, this was about them voting for it to make the headlines go away. I mean maybe, if you sat them down as people – outside of the House, politicians are people – a few of them would take this more seriously. But as politicians they just think, 'How do I make this thing go away? I need this constituent to stop writing to me; it's chaos.' That's the motivating factor, unfortunately.

Within five years of the change in the law, 20,000 UK adults were legally accessing medical cannabis through 'special prescribers'. The door now pushed ajar, other progressive changes have been made to reduce the harm caused by drugs. In 2022, the Home Office approved the UK's first drug testing service, following a City Council application, after Bristol experienced a spate of drug-related deaths caused by super-strength pills. The deputy mayor said he had been moved to act after witnessing how 'whole communities' are impacted when a young person's life is avoidably taken away.

Portugal, which decriminalised all drugs in 2001, adopted a public health approach in response to an epidemic in drug use in which one in every ten people had become a user. João Augusto Castel-Branco Goulão, the architect of Portugal's drug policy, has reflected that every family in the country, at the turn of the century, knew someone who had died of an overdose.

'I sometimes wonder if Portugal's approach is fully understood by people,' the drugs analyst Amber Moore tells me. Amber is Research Manager at User Voice and has a family history of opiate addiction.

'Portugal's problems with drugs were so severe, they kind of forced an alternative response. I sometimes think that people believe that decriminalisation of drugs is a kind of liberal thing to do when really it was in response to a serious problem they had and it seems to have been effective.'

Drug-related deaths have declined in Portugal since the turn of the century after placing emphasis on education and support in place of condemnation. Decriminalisation is quite a polarising term because it often gets falsely equated with legalisation, which it's not,' Amber continues. 'It just means drug possession is reduced to a civil offence, a bit like a driving offence.'

Although it's often not mentioned, decriminalisation in the way that Portugal's delivered it is synonymous with public health. Before they decriminalised, they invested very heavily in their drug treatment and prevention work as well. They didn't just decriminalise in law. So I think what is a shame is that when we talk about decriminalisation what we forget is that at the root of it is that public health investment and approach to it.

There will always be a case for policing – because unless you just legalise all drugs – which nowhere has done – then there's still going to be efforts to stop the illicit manufacture and trafficking of these drugs. But when we talk about low level drug use and social supply it's about having a completely different approach to that and that's where decriminalisation and public health models come in.

Amber's work at User Voice has a focus on influencing central government but she reflects that change in policy and practice actually tends to happens at the grass roots and happens 'despite' national policies. 'We have to think about what the goals are with drug policy reform. I think it should be that we have less harmful use, less deaths, less risky behaviours. Other people think it should be that we have no-one or very few people in society using drugs.'

'We need better data but there's little incentive for this government to provide better data if it's likely to show that the UK probably under-estimates drug use in the country by 20 per cent, because it makes it harder for the government to ignore it.'

Approaches to policing are increasingly devolved across the UK, however, meaning central government, again, do not need to represent an insurmountable roadblock to reform.

We are seeing drug-diversion schemes increasingly approved by police officers, where it is supported by local Police and Crime Commissioners. These PCCs have perhaps been inspired by the similar education and awareness schemes used in Portugal. Commissioners tend to dictate what some of the focuses should be for each police force and some are individuals, Chiefs of Police that have wanted to explore these alternatives to arrest. They haven't had to solicit a change in the law, they've been able to apply existing tools available to them, like Community Resolution orders.

Community Resolution orders for a while have been used to 'divert' people on to awareness and education courses for first offences of things like domestic abuse. There is evidence that these interventions can be effective if they are not delivered in a 'just say no to drugs kids' manner, which we know alienates people.

Research undertaken by User Voice into how drug diversion schemes can be best rolled out nationally promises to lead to less criminalisation for possession and less risky behaviour, building on the societal gains made by the rescheduling of cannabis for medical use. If the past fifty years have truly been characterised by failure, as North suggested, bolder and more bespoke approaches to advocacy appear to be consigning those days to the past.

CHAPTER NINE

ARTISTIC INTERVENTION – REALISING MENTAL HEALTH IN MEDIUM-SECURE HOSPITALS

Indefinite isolation is day-to-day reality for the thousands of patients diagnosed with mental illnesses cooped up in 60 medium-secure mental health hospitals dotted across England and Wales. The majority know neither when they will be discharged, nor what specifically they need to demonstrate in order to regain their liberty. I spent time with three patients just prior to the wider world falling under a desperate lockdown of its own as the Covid-19 pandemic hit.

Lucas – the Law of Attraction

'Let me hit you with this one,' Lucas challenges me. 'If I've got a piano.... If we've got a piano here, and a piano there, on the other side of the room.... If I hit the C-note on one piano, the string on the C-note on the other piano will vibrate too, without me touching it. Because it's in tune with the same frequency. And I believe whatever you attune yourself with, you can connect to.'

Lucas is in his early 20s, a restless amateur boxer with a one-step-ahead grin and sleepless eyes. His first words upon our meeting were to politely ask if we could carry out his own interview first, before I speak with his friends on the ward. He had 'other places' he needed to be soon. We are in a medium-secure hospital: there is a limit to how many destinations he has scope to experience today and all are within the grounds of this remote facility in the countryside. The hospital running club will assemble again tomorrow and it won't be exploring a new route. The astro-turf football pitch hasn't been booked. That's about it.

Lucas's brain is busier than he is, however. The Londoner doesn't like to sit still. His fellow patients are more than happy to let their friend speak first, to let the youngest one in the gang empty his mind a little. They have all afternoon to kill. Moreover, having just been 'subdued' by the post-lunch medication round, they are more accommodating than I'm told they might have been had I met them at a less benign hour than that deliberately selected by the hospital's NHS Trust press officer.

Lucas is a man in hurry today but he tells me this is not how he's always been.

'I was in a high-secure unit,' he recalls. 'So my life [back then] was pretty much over. And then something – a lot – happened on one day. It was a collection of coincidences and it set me down a path towards [subscribing to the theory of] the Law of Attraction: positivity and re-wiring the brain.'

The Law of Attraction is the belief that positive or negative thoughts bring positive or negative experiences into a person's life. The belief is based on the ideas that people and their thoughts are made from 'pure energy', and that a process of like energy attracting like energy exists through which a person can improve their health, wealth, and personal relationships.

Lucas is describing coming off nine months in seclusion at Ashworth, one of England's three High-Security Forensic Psychiatry Units. The 800 patients in these facilities live under the same conditions as those of Category B prisoners: i.e. those serving sentences of 10 years or more for whom 'escape needs to be made very difficult'. Suffice to say, sources of positive energy tend to be thin on the ground.

'I think it's widely recognised that there are a lot of people in prisons waiting for [mental health] beds,' Lucas' support worker says, her smile acknowledging how understated this will sound in print. 'Somebody can improve and they can start really engaging and, you know, settling in their mental health.'

Lucas continues: 'Three things then happened, all at the same time. My psychologist said something to me: I learned about ripple effects. Then I heard this thing "Law of Attraction" from [Mixed Martial Arts Champion] Conor McGregor.

'I then had this weird meditation, the first I've ever experienced.

'Bam bam bam.

'Then all of a sudden my friend sent me this book in: *The Key to the Law of Attraction*. It got censored by default.'

The sender was 'a complete random one; I hadn't heard from him for years. I'd just heard about [the Law of Attraction theory] the day before, then all of a sudden I'd got a book about it. I never asked for it! The key to living, it said: you gotta write goals. I thought, "Let me try that." Be positive. I want to better myself, get out of high-secure. And I did.'

'I started writing all these goals down. I kept ticking them off. Small things, big things. I keep ticking them still.'

It's rapid speech now. Having begun our conversation with blokey, fairly empty talk about boxing and Mixed Martial Arts fighting, Lucas has become more animated after switching lanes, expanding on the intersection between physics and philosophy.

Lucas credits the transformation of his prospects to taking ownership of his mindset, visualising a specific future for himself that once looked unthinkable after an experience involving an interaction with the criminal justice system that remains unnamed throughout our conversation.

The mentality shift was cemented under the mentorship of a German artist employed by Hospital Rooms, a charity that empowers in-patients to express themselves through artwork co-produced with professional artists that is then curated on the walls and corridors of unit wards.

'Lothar looks at buildings, these plain buildings, and then he visualises what he's trying to do,' explains Lucas. 'He sits there all day and you see him having a cup of tea, and he says he has to visualise it all, how it can look.'"

Together Lothar and Lucas collaborated on a sketch, a brush-stroke tribute made from black paint, of Conor McGregor, the revered professional fighter he'd referenced earlier. It carries the motif: 'I see something in my head, and then it happens.'

I ask Lucas what he visualises for himself. 'I have this dream in my head. It's not really a dream, it's a vision: I'm going to make it happen. I see it, I visualise it. I want to compete again, this year. I will fight in a competitive contest again this year. I'm due for release in a couple of months. You can't let other people's opinions stand in your way.'

Ashley: Mental Health Medication 'does not have to be pernicious to creativity'

Ashley is in his mid-thirties; welcoming, self-assured, immaculately presented, eloquent, calm, inventive, ambitious. He is also in a medium-secure hospital for the foreseeable future. The same hospital as Lucas, the boxer I have just met. And this is not the first such hospital that Ashley has spent time in.

The majority of psychiatric units are 'low-secure', promoting various freedoms while they treat patients in distress. These patients present a danger to themselves alone and a transient, moderate risk at that. Medium-secure hospitals, in contrast, operate in a similar fashion to Category B prisons. These institutions promise therapeutic intent also. But they are consciously designed with preventing escape as their overriding priority.

Everyone Ashley lives with on his locked ward has experienced some kind of 'interaction' with the criminal justice system (CJS). Many are prisoners who have been transferred to hospital as their mental health has deteriorated. Some have never been convicted of a crime but have arrived here having displayed diagnosed symptoms of mental illness during arrest or trial.

'I'm in here on an innocent verdict, but there was violence "around" the innocent verdict and that's why I got sectioned,' Ashley explains. The philosophy graduate distances himself from the profile of others receiving the same medical treatment and psycho-education he is receiving. 'Every day you're surrounded by people who are just talking about crime and drugs and you're just like, "Give it a rest," do you know what I mean?'

His hospital support worker, who lives with a bipolar disorder diagnosis herself, insists there is not one 'neat criteria' encompassing everyone who may be admitted for medium-secure care and supervision:

It's not like a lottery where you're the lucky ones who are going to hospital and not staying in prison. It's based on need. So if somebody is really presenting as acutely and severely in distress in a prison environment – and the prison cannot manage that level – and they need a higher level of mental health care, then the hospital environment may be better.

Prisons are very understaffed as well. If somebody is a real risk to themselves, then a prison environment is not necessarily the best place for them to be because they are locked in. So it's really based on need: who needs that bed.

Those on the outside who have never lived the experience form varying conclusions as to whether the environment will be received as soothing or suppressing based on what they have read, heard or seen as evidence or anecdote or absorbed first-hand on visits.

The NHS Trust press officer who has arranged the interview interjects to emphasise that it 'is not just about that [bed provision]. It is about treatment and recovery for the mental health issue as well. So while there is an element about them being in a secure unit so they can't leave and they don't have the limits on their freedom in that way, it is not just about that. It is about recovery and treatment for the illness that perhaps caused the offending, that led them to be involved with the criminal justice system.'

Only a tiny proportion of those embroiled in the CJS receive hospital treatment despite some claiming that virtually all prisoners live with diagnosable psychological needs. The fact that assessment of need is made by the government's justice secretary rather than the health secretary arguably demonstrates where the state's priorities still rest.

The context leaves staff having to make up their own minds as to whether they are treating or containing those they are ostensibly 'supporting'. Some are sympathetic, others are detached, but the mixed messages inevitably leave patients having to wrestle feeling disenfranchised at times.

Ashley finds his current care more therapeutic – 'much better' – than other hospitals he's been sectioned to in the past. However, such are the terms of Section 47 orders that you are obliged to show deference to the state's approach to your mental health. Section 47 orders last three months but they can be extended routinely if the patient doesn't demonstrate sufficient insight, even beyond the end date of a prison sentence.

A poem in Ashley's name that hangs from the wall depicts institutions as coercive, delivering 'alleviation from salvation'. I ask about the message. 'It's describing the infernal idiocy that you're stooped in most of the time and that [poem] was a reaction to that.'

Ashley, who has also published short stories and written film scripts, was encouraged to pursue his creative instincts by Hospital Rooms, the arts charity that supports patients to redesign areas of their ward in their own image.

The initiative and the approach to medication taken by Ashley's support worker have combined to give him renewed direction and faith in his future prospects, I'm told.

> I'm on fairly positive medication. I'm happy with it given my circumstances. Hospital Rooms inspired me to keep pushing my boundaries and limitations given the implications medication can have for creativity and that's been really a positive aspect [of the collaboration on the project].

Prior to meeting them, my drive for my artistic passions, even though it was there, it was less so that it is now, since them having been here.

Ashley apologies for his medication 'making it hard to speak' but he is articulate throughout our discussion. I ask whether, as an expressive person, he carries concerns about his treatment interfering with his ability to channel expansive ideas.

Not all medication acts that way. There are some medications that are actually quite helpful in that respect. The vast majority, I would say about at least 80 per cent, dependent on how you look at it, in terms of antipsychotics, are very pernicious to creativity. It gives you a general sense of lethargy. But on the whole, the other 20 per cent, if we can get into that category, they're very good.

What Hospital Rooms has taught me is that I can recreate the magic that they [showcased in workshops] on a smaller scale myself and then try to propagate that throughout the community in places such as this.

The most active way of me doing this is through the grant application process that they've schooled me in how to make. Hopefully that will come to fruition. There's no certainty. But if it does, then that will be an active means through which I'll get art out there.

Then once I get out into the community I'll be able to make grant applications and I've no policies to abide by and so there's the hope of me actually being able to fund myself and make a career as an artist at some level.

Adam: 'I've had psychosis before and recovered in months – I shouldn't be locked up for years'

'Half the staff agree with some of the patients here that it's excessive how long we're kept locked up,' I'm told. 'It doesn't take years to get better.' Adam is 6 feet 2 inches tall and broad shouldered but speaks softly. His morale is fragile after enduring four years of unbroken supervision in the medium-secure hospital where we've met.

Adam becomes enthused however when discussing his life 'outside'. Previously he had been working semi-professionally as a landscape artist. He has been painting since he was eight years old, when he practised tentative brushstrokes at his grandmother's water colouring society.

'For about five years we used to go to this big manor house. There were people painting in oils and other mediums. I spent a lot of time when I was younger there, with my grandma, painting. Fond memories....'

It feels the lifetime ago that it was. But every experience on the outside does. 'I've had various jobs: Vodafone, doing building work, working in pubs, bars and stuff. But I've always tried to make money from artwork.'

'I'm approaching four years [in hospital] and it's all off the back of what I'm accused of: assaulting a police officer.' Adam says he went to court five times, consistently pleading innocent to the charge. He maintains that his medical record, which included hospitalisations for psychosis [experiencing things that those around him were not able to see or hear], influenced the way he was treated by the criminal justice system and not for the betterment of his mental health.

Everyone Adam lives with on his ward has had one run-in or another with the CJS. By definition, that is the profile of patient his hospital – unlike most other psychiatric units – is there to treat (and contain). The mental health professionals working here hold a spectrum of views as to how they interpret their roles. For example, whether the individual or wider society are the priority of their work.

'I think half the staff are of the same opinion as some of the patients, whereby they think it's excessive how long that we're kept locked up and the other half think it's necessary,' Adam says, dispiritedly. 'There's a conflict of opinion there.'

'My solicitor said "Look, I know you believe you think you're innocent [but] you're better off just saying you're guilty and you'll get five months in prison and get out." So I should have taken her advice.'

Adam feels this way because he would have had his liberty restored by now, enabling him to see his daughter grow up. More than that though, he feels that pleading guilty to something 'I definitely didn't fucking do' would have spared him more of the diagnostic overshadowing [being judged on the basis of his mental health condition more than his actions] he says has been imposed on him perpetually since his arrest.

'I did eight months on remand in prison, which is longer than the sentence I would have got had I pleaded guilty. They then moved me to [a private mental health hospital] and a doctor who I spoke to there for three minutes went to court for my last appearance. They took the stand and said: "We believe he's very ill. He has a history of mental illness and we'd like to put him under section 37 / 41" [a particular detention for treatment in hospital]. They came to the conclusion that I didn't have the capacity to be tried because I wasn't pleading guilty and I've ended up doing a long time here.'

'I prefer prisons to be honest,' Adam continues, reflecting on the fleeting time he spent being assessed at the private hospital, where he wasn't under section, contrasting it with his current hospital, where he has resided without a single unescorted walk around the grounds' secure woodlands for four years. 'When you're in prison, your state of mind isn't being questioned.'

'What I'm trying to say is.... I'm not just complaining about my situation, but sometimes these places don't get it right. They get it totally "tits-up" and it just doesn't make any sense.'

Adam acknowledges Hospital Rooms, the arts charity offering creative outlets for patients, as the one therapeutic experience he's experienced since being transferred from prison to hospital. 'Things like Hospital Rooms are amazing. It gives the place a lot of hope. But at the same time, I think there are a lot of people locked up that don't need to be. It doesn't take years to get better.'

Adam recognises his own historic battles with psychosis but insists that 'lots of people end up in this situation and there's nothing wrong with them. I think.... I don't know.... Do you believe that?' he asks his support worker.

'I think it depends on the person,' flashes back the sincerely sensitive, though diplomatic, reply.

Adam initially seems to feel validated, but then swiftly becomes regretful at opening up.

'It depends on the person, yeah. Everyone's different. Sorry...! I'm banging on about.... I'm bringing it up, aren't I? What I've brought up, I'm trying to forget that, so apologies. Yeah, maybe I shouldn't bring it up. I don't know. I bring it up sometimes, don't I? I'll try not to. I need to move on. Move past that, sort of, yeah.'

His support worker encourages: 'I think you're working through it.'

'You need to get it off your chest,' I say.

'Yeah, I know. I didn't need to say that, to be honest. I don't know....' Adam turns to his friend Ashley, the patient I'd previously spoken to.

'What do you think, man? Honestly, these places, do they help?'

From what I've sort of seen and from what's happened to me through experience... as you said, it doesn't take years to get well. You can get someone who's unstable or someone who has just done something unusual and that's just a blip in their life and then they are locked up all this time.

They get well because they are here, *or* they get unwell, again. So it can be problematic, to be honest, being in this sort of situation, this environment, it can be very problematic. A lot of people can become institutionalised, but at the same time, for a lot of people, it can be a positive thing.

The ambivalence hangs in the air and it is clearly felt heavily by the patients and the support worker they share.

'I've been in hospital quite a few times in the past on "section threes",' Adam adds. 'I had a few psychotic episodes when I was younger [and] recovered within months. In the latter years of being in hospital it, hospital, feels very unnecessary.'

Adam thinks a lot about his family: his grandmother who introduced him to watercolours, his daughter, his parents. He continues to enter his artwork for competitions while waiting indefinitely for progress towards discharge. Prizes are forwarded on to his mother and father for safekeeping. A bottle of Champagne awarded by the global law firm Dentons, for his watercolour depiction of 'Three camels walking towards a desert oasis', is among those waiting for him at his parents' house .

Material from this chapter first appeared on Mental Health Today *and is re-published with permission. Names have been changed to preserve anonymity.*

CHAPTER TEN

PALESTINE'S 'WALL MUSEUM' – BREAKING DOWN BARRIERS

Yara van Teeffelen was still a primary school pupil when she entered the claustrophobic granite checkpoint guarded by Israeli soldiers in Bethlehem, the Palestinian's city of birth.

She remembers girls and women losing their rings and earrings in the metal detectors. 'They [the soldiers] wouldn't give them baskets, so people would have to place them inside, on the machine. All the rings would get stuck in the machine and they wouldn't give a shit about it, they would just continue on like, "It's your problem".'

Yara's Christian family have always loathed the indignity and uncertainty that accompanies any attempt to negotiate the border checkpoint, but the holy city of Jerusalem remains Palestine's capital city despite its occupation. The 740km (460-mile) wall erected in 2002 was done so by Israel illegally, according to the International Court of Justice.

'It was Easter time,' recalls Yara's mother, Mary. They attempted the journey that day with Toine, Mary's husband. Toine is Yara's father and holds a Dutch passport. 'A friend of mine called me to ask him to bring the kids for chocolate egg hunting and so on, for them to enjoy the Easter holiday.'

'We went to the checkpoint to cross to Jerusalem and the woman soldier wanted Yara, who was nine years old, to take down her pants.' Yara resisted all strip-search attempts. 'I was angry. She was only nine years old... why take off her clothes? There were people there. I started saying "No, no, no". They refused to let us pass and so we went back home.'

Palestinians are often remarked upon for their resilience. Not long after returning home, Mary determined once again that she would deliver the Easter experience that had been intended. 'I'm a bit stubborn, so I said I want to go with the kids, for them to enjoy and see something with friends. We took the bus – which we are not allowed to take – from Bethlehem to Jerusalem.'

'" was honest with the bus driver, saying that we had to go to Jerusalem and so on. He said, "I don't know if you will pass, but let's try." We took the bus, me and the kids, and by luck only, the woman soldier didn't see our identity. But we arrived late for the egg hunt. It was over, unfortunately.'

As Mary concludes the story, she laughs. Here in particular it remains better to laugh than to cry and Palestinians possess rare stoicism, sometimes referred to as *sumud*. Palestinians are prevented from travelling freely around Israel and yet some 500,000 Israeli settlers have made the West Bank their home without pushback from successive governments.

'There's so much anger [but] also different types of emotion,' explains Mary's husband, Toine. 'People also try to adapt. Many try to look in other directions to avoid what is happening in front of you: the humiliation. It's difficult being humiliated all the time, so better to think about other things.'

'Also, people who pass the checkpoint, they isolate themselves from their environment, so they can feel as if they are not being influenced by the faces, by the gestures, the sounds of the soldiers. This is one way to protect yourself and your dignity.'

Toine has facilitated another way, too. An anthropologist by background, the Dutchman has curated cathartic release for Palestinians through empowering his wife and dozens of other survivors – of what is increasingly recognised as apartheid – to document their human rights violations and display them in the most defiant of locations. The checkpoint experience endured by the family has been immortalised as a story for public view, presented framed behind perspex – alongside 250 other testimonies – nail-gunned to the 9m (30-foot) high wall that divides Israel and Palestine.

Toine has been supporting Palestinians to be heard for decades. The approach has been honed with increasing poignancy throughout his career at the Arab Educational Institute. The organisation delivers training in human rights advocacy to Palestinians.

'It gives some strength, inner strength – we call it *sumud* – to see your story being read by others,' he says.

> Twenty years ago, in the wake of the second intifada [uprising against Israel] we had researchers from universities and students collecting stories, but we never knew what happened with them, whether they had any impact, or whether they were purely analysed.
>
> However, with the Wall Museum stories, seeing *visually* people standing in front of the wall reading them... that

has been impacting in the sense that you *really know* that your story is being read.

We want people to have more understanding of the lack of freedom for Palestinians in the area, the impact of the wall, the fact that people cannot travel easily into Jerusalem, also the whole permit system, that people need a permit in order to go into Israel. These were the main messages.

That people are locked up in ghettos is a very basic thing for people abroad to know. From birth, people don't have the vision, the vista, that they can be free in their own country. That is the very basic message.

We had this idea of putting the stories on the wall because at the Institute we had a tradition of working with stories. Sometimes we brought visitor groups to our 'story house' there, next to the wall. Then at one point we decided, 'why don't we put our posters on the wall, so that more people can see it?'

We already had a good documentation of Palestinian women in their daily life, stories... strange stories of human rights... also stories of Muslims and Christians living together, which is an important message because pilgrims to Bethlehem often don't know that there are Palestinian Christians.

I ask Mary who she would like to read her story. 'The whole world,' she replies.

Mary refers back to the bleak checkpoint experience with her daughter. 'They were humiliating people. There was a room where the soldier wanted you to go. They would ask you to go there.'

'There was a women in there, a Palestinian lady, and they asked her to take off her clothes until she was almost naked. Now, they don't do that any more. I'm sure people complained and I'm sure they know that it's not right, what they are doing.'

Could the poster created by Mary have contributed to the change in practice?

'We know that in 2016, in the middle of the night, soldiers came to check the stories,' Toine says. "We know that from one of the people who lived near them. One of the soldiers was reading the posters in English and another was translating the posters into Hebrew. A third one was putting it onto an audio tape. So it seemed that they were interested to know what the content of the stories was and whether it was a case of 'incitement' or not.

Mary's poster was not removed. One referencing 'Apartheid Road' was taken down, though the majority have proven as enduring as the Palestinian community of Bethlehem itself.

The impact of the Wall Museum on Israeli security forces should not be overstated, Yara believes. 'They get trained not to have that empathy and not to feel much when they are on duty.'

'I think life will change but not during my time, adds Mary. 'It will take maybe 100 years, maybe less."' The family's sense of humour is not defeated. 'There was a joke that it won't change, even in God's lifetime,' Toine says.

The posters are aimed at international guests. 'We have had some people say we should put posters on the other side of the wall,' Toine explains. 'The goal was really to influence the attitudes of pilgrims and tourists coming in to Bethlehem. Israelis cannot see the posters because they are not allowed to enter "Area A" so the aim is rather on the level of the public opinion of visitors.'

'We always see groups passing by, reading them or taking pictures, so we know it really has had an impact on public opinion, for groups coming into Bethlehem. Our Wall Museum is not far from the Banksy hotel, "The Walled Off".' The British graffiti artist opened the art gallery hotel in 2017. It is an immersive museum documenting the history of Palestinian resistance. A replica hotel has recently opened its doors in Paris.

'There are also Palestinian guides, who guide visitors along the wall – geo-political tours, they call them – to show visitors the Palestinian story.'

'Sometimes we see Americans who are pro-Palestinian,' says Mary. 'I think America is an evil, but there are some who care and also some from Europe who care.' Israel receives 80 per cent of its arms imports from America but the administration of Joe Biden expressed 'serious concern' in 2023 at mandated expansion of settlements in the West Bank.

'The political battlefields will be in the US,' Toine says. 'In the past, Palestinians were more often associated with terrorism. The Democratic Party has really changed now. If that is going to continue then that might really make a change in the situation.'

Toine is not holding out for a groundswell of sympathy from Europe. 'There has always been a very strong blockade, an emotional blockade, and part of that stems from the Second World War. I can't say that has completely changed but yes, more people have been open to Palestinian reality than in the past. I think in general, the situation of daily life is more known here than in the past. But on the political level, the governmental level, it hasn't changed that much.'

It would be 'the very worst type of analysis' to suggest there is any prospect of international momentum propelling Palestinian freedoms forward, Toine insists. We are speaking six months prior to the multiple horrors that unfolded in Israel and Palestine in October 2023. 'Of course, you are hopeful. There's also no time for despair. When you live here, things go on, we try to bring our humanity to do what we want, to do what we can.'

The Wall Museum has shown that Palestinians can write their own realities. There are legacies if you look for them. Since graduating with degrees in both Political Design and Interaction Design in Holland, Yara has returned to the country of her birth to take up a role at an organisation empowering marginalised communities.

The 25-year-old describes one of the imaginative innovations she has conceived at the NGO. It's luxury confectionery, made by Palestinian women who lost their jobs during the Covid-19 pandemic. The sweet packaging is designed to live a second life, 'as a sculpture, something that you can hang, something of beauty'. Like the posters of the Wall Museum, these sculptures also amplify narratives. In this case, they contain the back-stories of each of the women who created the sweets.

Says Yara: 'I was born in Palestine and I have been living back here since the end of the pandemic. Before that I was living in the Netherlands, where I did my bachelor's degree and my master's degree.

'Coming back to Bethlehem, it changed the way I viewed the city. I somehow became more aware of the situation than when I was here. When I left Bethlehem I was 17 years old. Back then, being surrounded by a wall didn't sound so absurd. It was just something I was born "in" and with.'

The wall is twice the size of that which used to run through Berlin, dividing Western Europe and the former Soviet Union. 85 per cent of the granite structure sits inside the West Bank. There are over 100 different permits restricting freedom of movement for Palestinians. The Easter trips to see friends that the majority of society take for granted remain as problematic as ever for Palestinians.

'I started putting things in perspective only when I came back. Because when you are abroad then of course you are free to do whatever you want. You are not restricted, not limited in the ways of travel, in ways of expressing yourself.'

'The moment you come back to the country you see how big a difference it actually is. Despite the political situation, I came back to live here in Bethlehem because I wanted to bring back the knowledge I gained in Europe and in the West.' Yara reformulates her thoughts: 'Not necessarily bring it back here but somehow try and find the things that I can improve with the knowledge that I gained over there.'

In other words, the experience affirmed once again to Yara that she should not limit herself or be controlled, despite the imposing, dehumanising security services and shadow-forming structures that loomed over her as a child.

'But with that, I also realised lots of cultural difference that I truly missed when I was abroad. The people, the sense of hospitality, the food, the weather, the culture – it's more welcoming here than in Europe. Besides the political situation and the harsh reality that we live in, despite all of that, we do feel closer as a people, as among the Palestinian people there's more bonding, more connection between each other; the families are more connected.'

Inner strength and stoicism. Reinforced through defiance published on the very walls built to break it.

PART FIVE

PEACE: AUTONOMY, AMBITION AND 'VENTILATION'

CHAPTER ELEVEN

PATHS TO INDEPENDENCE – ETA PRISONER BECOMES LEADER'S LEGAL ADVISER

Gonzalo Boye is an enigma. One of the most respected, in-demand human rights lawyers in Spain, the Chilean is simultaneously synonymous with an an ETA kidnapping for which he was sent to jail.

The millionaire attorney is best known for protecting Catalan independence leader Carles Puigdemont from extradition from Belgium to Spain, where he remains wanted on charges including sedition for organising a breakaway referendum unsanctioned by Madrid.

Yet bespectacled chain-vaper Boye carries a heavy criminal record. He spent eight years in jail when found guilty by a panel of three judges of participating in the planning of an abduction.

Boye went on to study law from his cell – earning his professional credentials in the least credible or professional setting – having earlier dropped out of a German university without graduating.

Terror charges in Spain are handled by the country's Audiencia National court and are not subject to trial by jury. Boye was sentenced in 1995 without any recourse to appeal.

'When you are convicted [and sentenced] to 15 years in prison, for something that has happened when you are not in the country, then something is wrong,' Boye tells me. 'Something went wrong and in order to understand what went wrong, I really needed to study the whole legal system. There was nothing wrong with the law. It was the application of the law [that was flawed].'

Emiliano Revilla was held hostage for eight months before a 12 million dollar ransom was paid. He made no accusation against Boye. Similarly, ETA made no suggestion that Boye had played a role.

Boye has accused Spanish police of torture following his arrest and he believes the conviction was politically motivated. 'We have people who use the law to repress others. These people say we are a democracy and take pride in the constitution but then use the law for their own purposes and this hasn't changed in the the last 30 years.'

'People say we need change. What we need to change is the mentality of the people who use the law for their own purpose.

'The prosecution service makes a proposal, but the parties that apply the law in Spain are the judges and courts and they have to understand that the courts are there to respond to the rule of law and not to political interventions.'

At the time of our interview, in May 2023, Boye is in the dock again, this time accused of money laundering. The corruption charges first surfaced in 2019, the year of Spain's 'trial of the century', when all the leaders of Catalonia's independence – save for Puigdemont – were tried for treason for their involvement in the referendum.

I reported on that trial from Spain. I met with Ignacio Juradao, a politics professor at King Carlos III University in Madrid. 'There are a lot of accusations in Spain that the judiciary's actions are articulated by the Spanish government,' he told me. 'I don't believe this and I believe the judicial system is independent. But being independent doesn't mean being apolitical. The judges in the Supreme Court have their own ideology. We have a judicial system that tends to be right wing and the sense of state obedience is quite embedded within it.'

Ultimately, nine of the 12 accused received prison sentences for the crime of sedition. Of these, four were also found guilty of misuse of public funds. Their sentences ranged from nine to 13 years. The remaining three accused were found guilty of disobedience and fined.

While the left were defeated, the separatist uproar – which involved scores of mass protests – did coincide with some unprecedented self-reflection in parliament's corridors of power. A shrine to former dictator Francisco Franco, which had remained incongruously at the Valley of the Fallen monument to the victims of Spain's civil war, was finally removed from the landmark, a move authorised by the prime minister.

Franco's dictatorship emerged following the Nationalists' victory over the Republicans in the Spanish civil war fought in the 1930s. Spain constructed a well-intentioned policy of amnesty and silence 'to heal' during the transition to democracy as Franco died. However, peace is fragile and contingent on faith in each individual and region (or nation) of Spain being treated equally.

Boye reflects with me on how matters came to a head in Catalonia in recent years. 'First the Spanish central government let Catalans think that they were going to be able to change their situation, through a new statute within Spain. Once the assembly parliament approved it, then the right-wing parties challenged that decision in the constitutional court and the constitutional court ripped it up.'

'That was all controlled by the right-wing parties, they squashed the new legal frame for the Catalans. In this moment, Spain was showing and telling Catalans that if they don't go to the streets then they will get nothing because what was promised was not fulfilled. Catalonia decided to make a referendum. The state said "No". At the end, they did it anyway and once they did it... the repression that followed, we all saw it.'

Human Rights Watch documented excessive use of force against peaceful demonstrators by civil guards or national police officers at a primary school in Girona being used as a polling station and in surrounding hillside villages, too.

Catalonia's Health Department estimated that on the day following the October 1st referendum in 2017, some 893 people reported injuries to the authorities. Meanwhile, Spain's ministry of the interior said 33 members of the police and civil guards had required urgent medical assistance.

'Five years after the referendum they are still repressing the Catalans and everyone around them,' continues Boye. 'That's not creating the right atmosphere to have a dialogue and a political situation – this is only creating more mutual hate.'

'This also happened in Chile. During Pinochet's time, some people became very rich and some people became poor. Then it went back to democracy in 1990 and people were expecting certain changes which politicians had offered and promised them. Twenty years after that nothing had happened and on top of that they were having their fundamental rights restricted. So the people went to the streets. In the context of Chile it was a violent reaction, but it was also a violent repression. It was like two trains crashing, one into the other.'

However, far from feeling defeated, the 58-year-old Boye is convinced, from watching bottom-up movements in both his native Chile and what he calls the 'minority nations' of Spain, that it is within these very circumstances of repression that social change breakthroughs tend to occur.

The transcendent equation, Boye says, is 'repression added to social and economic inequality... the population acts like a gas: you can compress it up to a moment where it explodes.'

'We are human beings. If you take an individual and start pushing him against the wall, that person will either let themselves be squashed or they will react. Well, with social movements, it happens the same way. The people, as a mass, it is almost the same.'

When I ask Boye what the Catalan protesters have achieved that they can be most proud of, he points to their non-violence, saying it has won them their legitimacy in their current battle for greater autonomy from Spain. However he argues that violence, in some circumstances, can be justified. Boye points to confrontations with dictators such as Franco and Pinochet in Chile to illustrate his argument.

'I hate violence, but I understand that in certain moments of history, there is no other option but violence. I mean if you are shooting me, what should I do? There is no other option than violence. If you are shooting me, should I come out of the trench and say, "Let's talk? Let's discuss it?"'

Boye argues ETA – the once feared but now disarmed Basque separatist group – 'played an historical role in the 1960s and 1970s' fighting Franco. 'There was a moment of confrontation. It was a horrible and brutal dictatorship and there was a moment to confront it. And you can confront it; all means are valid in a confrontation with a dictatorship. After a dictatorship falls it becomes a different issue. This sort of organisation will always take a very long time to develop a new political position that allows them to change the means. They didn't change the objective, they changed the means.'

> I haven't participated. I was dragged into that conflict by the Spanish police. At that time I didn't have a single unit of knowledge of that conflict. But when you go into the roots of the conflict, the roots are a centralised country that wants to 'drag' all the nationalities. There are two peoples: Catalans and Basques. And there is a third one called Spaniards. Here there is a conflict between two small nationalities – two national minorities – confronted with an imperialist nationality, which is the Spanish, who are not accepting that they lost the Empire.

> ETA lasted too long in my opinion and in the end that made it very difficult for a political solution for the Basque Country. There remains no political solution until now but they are gaining room and gaining more self-government and maybe one day they will be able to go into an independence referendum, like in Scotland for example.

With violence there was nothing to be discussed, that's what the Spanish said. Until now, in Catalonia, without violence there is still nothing to be discussed, but at least the Catalans have got the legitimacy to continue fighting for their rights. And the Basques, since ETA disappeared, are gaining legitimacy for their claims.

The Basque Country and Catalonia are totally different to the rest of Spain economically because of their 'proximity way' of doing business, which means that they are self-sufficient; they don't need anybody to survive.

For example, and by way of comparison, if I want to have a salad in Madrid, the salad's ingredients will not have come from Madrid. The lettuce is coming from one part of Spain, the tomatoes are coming from another part, the onion from another. So when last year there was a lorry strike we didn't have any salad in Madrid, but that didn't affect Catalonia or the Basque Country. Why? Because they have a different way of sustaining their economy and it works and that's something that they appreciate.

Despite their grievances at paying more in tax than they receive in fiscal spending, both the Basque Country and Catalonia have won increasing self-governance and both are recognised as economic powerhouses across Europe.

In 2019, the year Madrid's courts were sending Catalonia's independence leaders to jail, the region generated a GDP of 250,597 million Euros, representing more than 20 per cent of Spain's total GDP and exceeding the European Union's average GDP by 12 per cent. The same year Bilbao, a metropolis in the Basque

Country, stood out as the only 'Spanish' city to feature in the top 20 of the inaugural global 'inclusive prosperity' index. The status was realised 42 years after the end of fascism in Spain and eight years after ETA formally committed to end its campaign of non-violence.

'ETA went through a process of political maturity. They reached a moment where they thought "it's not right, what we're doing, it's not useful any more, we have to change the means," and they abandoned the army wheels and started using the political wheels, which was extremely correct.'

When I ask Boye to identify the influences that have had the biggest bearing on his socio-political outlook as it stands today, he spends some time contemplating his time in prison, but dwells for longer when discussing his parents:

> I spent part of my eight years in prison, a very important part of it, in isolation. I used the time to study, to read, to play sport and to think, 'What do I want to do when I come out and how do I want to do it?' And what I decided to do is what I am doing now. I'm a product of those eight years. I learned to understand what inequality is, what unfairness is and what injustice is.
>
> The law is nothing but a tool to solve problems, not to create new problems.
>
> I don't know who I would be today if I didn't suffer that injustice but I have an approximate view of how it would be. Maybe my life would have been easier but I have doubts that it would be different, because when I went to prison, though I was a young adult, I had already received very good information from my parents and my school.

My mother was right-wing and my father was left-wing. We were brought up in a context of dictatorship in Chile, us as children, but my parents were brought up in a context of democracy [Boye's mother moved to Chile from Catalonia], so they couldn't accept and they didn't understand.

My parents told us always about the values of democracy and the values of dialogue, including accepting discrepancy. Sometimes I have the impression that the biggest illness in Spain is that they are not capable of accepting discrepancy. I have a lot of friends who are extremely right-wing and a lot of friends who are extremely left-wing. I try to put them together in my house sometimes. That's how I was brought up.

CHAPTER TWELVE

PSYCHOSOCIAL FOR THE SAHEL – QUELLING VIOLENT EXTREMISM IN WEST AFRICA

❛I remember many years ago when I used to hear about suicide bombs in Afghanistan and Middle Eastern countries I would be like, "Wow, how are they surviving?"' recalls Nigerian counsellor and peacebuilder Mary Hwyere, speaking down the line from long-troubled Borno. It's the state that gave rise to Boko Haram in north-east Nigeria.

Fast-forward to the present day and Hwyere has now supported more than 5,000 female survivors of terror, along with many men. This has been delivered through her role leading the work delivered by International Alert, an NGO, on social cohesion, reconciliation and reintegration for those that escaped Boko Haram captivity.

The Islamist group's name translates as 'Western Education is Forbidden'. Their structure had reached a crossroads by the time of our conversation in 2021, with some fighters folding into the forest bases of Islamic State (Isis) following the death of their movement's feared leader Abubakar Shekau.

Shekau introduced the now internationally notorious tactics of abductions and armed violence following the death of his predecessor, Mohammed Yusuf, who was killed while in police custody in 2009. A critical moment in Nigeria's recent history, it followed the failure of multiple government efforts to shut down the movement he had founded seven years earlier.

Boko Haram was 'more or less peaceful' under its first leader, Hwyere says. 'Yusuf started a religious complex and school that a lot of people came to. They were the rich and poor, but mostly they were the poor. His teachings appealed to their sense of reasoning or to their religion.'

'Yusuf talked about bad governance in the country, he talked about corruption. People were going through a lot – are still going through a lot – of poverty. There's feelings of injustice, feelings of marginalisation, between or among the people.'

Yusuf's death was not received well by many, though what followed seemed to take the country's authorities by surprise.

'After he was killed, very little was said about Yusuf's followers, not knowing that they were to prepare for revenge. It was Abubakar Shekau who took over. He came out more violent.' Boko Haram became ruthless, 'attacking people in the market, in the bus stations... anywhere where there's a crowd of people, they capitalised on that.'

Within five years the group had claimed power across seven regions (LGAs) of Africa's most populous country, while provoking outrage and despair for its sexual enslavement of abductees.

Confronted with such atrocities, promises to sweep Boko Haram away proved popular at the ballot box. Muhammadu

Buhari, Nigeria's two-term president until 2023, was voted in on a mandate to 'crush' the insurgency within months of taking office. The restoration of security in the north east was a key pillar of his campaign.

Supplies were cut off and the army became more forceful in repelling their adversaries. 'People were really tired of the killings, the disruption, the loss of lives and property. That seemed to be real hope from hopelessness. And by 2016 he was seemingly winning the fight by claiming those LGAs back.'

'That was really commendable... people were really happy the government were fighting terror.' But Hwyere smiles wryly in recalling a government claim from the time that the war on terror had been 'won'.

As in 2009, the Boko Haram of 2016 licked its wounds before re-emerging even more vengeful, now targeting humanitarian workers for the first time. Meanwhile, another government approach, incentivising fighters to surrender in return for grants to initiate business enterprises, has also brought mixed returns.

'It has really caused a lot of grievances among communities who were displaced. There's no form of compensation from the government, so they are feeling that "We are the victims, but the perpetrators are being rewarded for the crimes they committed."'Some of those feeling neglected see ransom banditry as a route to "a free square meal."'

A sense of unfairness, when combined with prevailing poverty and lack of government support, has seen violent uprisings perpetuate across the globe. Injustices, oppression, and lack of government support are some of the factors that drive people to follow violent approaches, or Jihad, risk reduction specialists explain.

In neighbouring Mali, the breadth of the security threats faced by a country that has experienced multiple coups in recent years weighs heavily on its people.

Oumar Arby, who until recently managed Alert's local peace-building programmes from Bamako, lists no less than seven extremist factions that have been active in his country for over a decade: JNIM, Islamic State West Africa (ISWA), Islamic State Greater Sahara (ISGS), Al Qaeda in the Islamic Maghreb (AQIM), Al Mourabitoun, Ansar Dine, and Katiba Macina.

Impatience at the glacial implementation of ready-to-go policies to support the farmers, herders and fishers whose water-dependent vocations have been compromised by climate change has been key. Frustration has been ignited by easily accessible weaponry, involving arms imported down into the Sahel after the collapse of Libya.

'It is essential for the Malian state to identify the reasons for the attractiveness of the ideological extremists and the political and economic dimensions of their actions, which have undeniably brought them the support of some groups within the population,' says Arby.

'The situation has forced some communities to arm themselves for self-protection. A comprehensive approach to improve security and fight terrorism, alongside efforts to protect civilians and restore both state authority and basic social services is needed from the Malian state and its international partners.'

Terror's power exists, of course, through the perceptions it creates. Videos circulating demonstrate both the arms and ambitions in play. Hwyere is just one of the millions of Nigerians sometimes kept awake at night by foreboding at what the future holds for their country, having witnessed the path to stability take one step forwards then two steps back, with many of the prevention measures adopted at state level to date.

'Here in the north east, you will not find one person who has not been affected directly or indirectly by this insurgency; this terrorism,' Hwyere says. 'Either someone has lost a daughter through these things, a friend, or a neighbour. Or they have lost their livelihood, their business, their source of income. So people are living with hatred.

Hwyere's colleagues build peace by confronting the trauma Nigeria's north is living with, applying psychosocial techniques to erode sufferers' yearning to repay their pain. We have support sessions aimed at helping people. In psychology, they call it "ventilation".'

'We try to hear what their mindsets are, what they are feeling. They express bitterness, they express grievances, they become wild and they [also] cower over littler things. So that shows they are really traumatised. And some of them just want revenge. You have people who do not want to forgive, so if they are put in a position where they can kill the person, they will.'

'Different simulations are constructed to demonstrate forgiveness. The facilitator takes some stones and asks everyone to put them in their shoes and walk around for ten minutes – you can imagine how it feels. So the message is that if you carry "unforgiveness", you are the one who is hurting.'

Hwyere highlights one group fighting for power in Nigeria, the Fulani militias, as having had particular recruitment success recently in praying on traumatised men, emphasising the role psychosocial services must continue to play as the country adapts to threats beyond Boko Haram.

'We had another practical session. We had a glass of Coke and a bottle of water. The Coke is like our state of mind, which is so darkened with pain, with regret, with "unforgiveness". Then a bottle of water is poured over the glass. Over time the glass starts changing colour until it become clear.'

'The participants see the need to forgive and to let go.'

Material from this chapter first appeared on the International Alert website and is re-published with permission.

CHAPTER THIRTEEN
'NO COMPROMISE' – COLOMBIA FINDS ITS PEACE MAP

I visited Colombia in 2004. The country had just reached its kidnapping 'peak'. Within hours, my taxi had been pulled over by a truck containing 20 men in green and brown fatigues. Most were stood on the back of the vehicle, holding guns the same height as the militiamen themselves. It was unclear whether they represented Farc – the revolutionary armed forces of Colombia – or one of Colombia's multiple other armed factions. My driver and I were body searched. We were waved on our way after I showed my passport. I breathed a sigh of relief. I remember, the following day, seeing a carrier bag of cocaine being merrily walked down the street as if it were a sack of groceries.

I anticipated experiences like this before I arrived, though perhaps not so immediately upon arrival. After I left, I followed Colombia's fortunes from afar. Insecurity perpetuated in the papers and the international pages of news sites. Drugs dominated headlines. It felt like Colombia would always exist as I had remembered it. But then suddenly, serious talk emerged of a peace agreement being struck between Farc and the Colombian government. And then in 2016, an accord was signed between the parties in Havana, Cuba's capital.

Emilio Archila, a patient and optimistic lawyer, was appointed soon after as the man tasked with delivering the first promises of the peace deal. It had already been recognised with a Nobel prize. But at this stage the accord was merely a plan on a piece of paper. I was intrigued by Archila. I was compelled to hear how Colombia had turned its fortunes around and wanted to learn how its new 'governor for stabilisation' intended to maintain the momentum. We arranged an interview.

Archila is from Bogota, the capital of Colombia. He was born in 1964. The same year, Farc was founded in the surrounding mountains as the military wing of the Communist party. Archila watched the Farc, over half a century, recruit child soldiers and kidnap thousands of civilians for ransom.

The country had endured sustained violence before the foundation of Farc. But not like this. Fuelled by 20,000 fighters, Farc became the largest armed insurgency in the world and became chiefly responsible for Colombia gaining a global reputation for danger. The country became a narco-state. Indiscriminate explosions and abductions made life and travel within the country an anxiety-inducing nightmare.

I ask Archila what lessons he has learned that can give hope to others living through divisions and conflict when they are experienced in the moment as intractable. In stilted English he invokes what his country's politicians were told by their counterparts from Germany during the state visit of a delegation led by Angela Merkel, the former Chancellor, eight years earlier.

'The Germans have a lot of experience "getting over" difficult challenges. They told us, we are here to help you, but we are here to help you in your own way.'

Each conflict is unique, but there are three common threads that unite their resolution, Colombia's future peacebuilders were told. 'First, the conflict resolvers must think large: dream that you can really change the next generation. Then you need to go for the huge prize and not be satisfied with anything less than the whole piece. Finally, you must understand that no-one will notice when success has been achieved. When a conflict is overcome, success is evidenced by the fact that *nothing is happening*. People are going to school or work, and in the background, *nothing is happening*.'

Archila emphasises that social change, when it is truly achieved, is not accompanied by a climactic soundtrack. 'There is no cheering during the moments when you know you have truly succeeded because of how it all looks – people are merely going to school; going to work.'

Colombia has not fully arrived at that place yet. It is not anticipated to round off its journey until the latter half of the 2030s. The terms of the peace agreement signed in 2016 are being implemented as a cross-party movement over four presidential terms. Colombia has seen armistices undone by the cycle of elections under previous administrations and Archila believes disrupting politics' traditional dynamics of competition in favour of a commitment to long-term cross-party collaboration are key when attempting to execute profound change.

'It takes more than the four years of a government term to agree and implement the solutions to everything on the "to do" list of the 2016 peace agreement. Many of the items within the accord are not very innovative because they are merely reflecting what has been diagnosed in the past. However what is different now is that the constitutional court has given us four terms to implement what has been diagnosed after every armistice we have had in the past (and we have had a lot of armistices here in Colombia).'

Even in the first term, Colombia had already made more progress on building peace than in the previous 50 years combined. Farc has disarmed and handed its weapons over to the United Nations. Alternative vocations in sectors ranging from fish farming to tourism have been and continue to be created, each enterprise co-designed by two ex-combatants in tandem with two lawyers.

Farc were given six guarantees by the Colombian government under the terms of the 2016 peace plan: economic sustainability, family reunion, health, education, housing and psychological reintegration. However, the most ambitious policy, and the one that is of most importance to the wider population, relates to a one billion peso compensation award to victims. This figure equates to three times the state budget for rail and road. Each and every policy needs to be fulfilled in order for Colombia to arrive at its potential as a country of lasting peace. Will it?

Gerard Martin is a peace monitor based in the mountainous Colombian city of Medellin, observing implementation of the Colombian peace accord on behalf of the Kroc Institute for International Peace Studies headquartered in the Netherlands. I speak to Martin in 2022, three years into the second of these four-year administrations.

'Looking at many indicators you see enormous improvements,' Martin begins, pointing to the number of people who fled the most dangerous villages around Medellin before Farc disarmed who have now started to return. 'Forced displacements have gone down. Forced disappearances have gone down. Kidnappings are almost zero. Illegal mining that had gone up is now down since Farc became inactive. Overall the peace agreement and the Farc moving out of their armed struggle into politics has been a major improvement for Colombia.'

Martin reinforces Archila's claims pertaining to the scale of ambition shown by Colombia's peacemakers, pointing out that the accord contains more commitments – 578 – than each of the other 34 peace agreements his institute monitors.

> People say the commitment to bringing the drug economy to an end has only progressed 20 per cent, but the peace accord's commitment agrees to do this over 20 years, which is four or five government terms. So it could only ever progress 20 per cent in this initial phase. The commitments related to disarmament, demobilisation and reintegration of former combatants have made significant progress, but again that's because many of these commitments had to be delivered in the first six months.

> The important thing is to maintain a constructive interpretation. If the conflict has lasted so long it's because there are complex factors behind it. There's no doubt that governments can work faster and more efficiently but we should not only make assessments in terms of political will.

> The research department for forced disappeared people is also delivering strong technical work that is making progress. It is going to take 10-15 years and thank God because there's tens of thousands of forced disappeared people. This is a slow and very sophisticated process and so we have to install ourselves. In our reports it's always

the central argument that the best way to go forward is to go forward with the peace agreement as it was agreed to.

Martin lived in Medellin at a time when homicides were as high as any city in the world and has seen many of the surrounding region's burned out farms with his own eyes. Like Archila he believes Colombia has turned a corner through refusing to compromise in the scale of its ambition, while also building in sufficient time and collaboration to empower a plan that will last the course. In fact, Martin believes the foundations were built far earlier than 2016.

'The reforms that the peace accord commits to have to also be understood in this larger context of Colombia trying to pacify its society. Colombia is still a very centralised country but the constitution of 1991 did do something in the direction of bringing state institutions closer to the people, including in the rural areas.'

Farc were born out of a desire for decentralised power. With many of their former fighters now sitting in parliament or running their own enterprises, some may claim that Farc have shaped Colombia's future more than those who might claim to have placated the group. What perhaps can't be denied is that each party needed the other in order to unlock the scope of their ambitions.

PART SIX

CONFOUNDING REPRESSION, PUNCTUATING PARANOIA

CHAPTER FOURTEEN
ALBANIA, OUT OF THE SHADOWS – SOFT-POWER HISTORICISING

Former interrogation rooms, secret surveillance labs and nuclear bunkers are being opened up to the public, exposing and acknowledging hidden horrors endured as Albania cut itself adrift across four decades. The Balkan state wants to show how far it has changed, believing this creative approach will strengthen its hand in negotiations to become a member of the European Union.

'For most Albanians, it has always been our dream to join the EU,' Etleva Demollari explains gently. The personal yearning of this museum director and mother began while growing up in 1980s Tirana. Her city had become the poorest capital in the world at the time: communism's biggest economic failure and a reflection of self-defeating isolationism.

Demollari used to watch Italian TV stations through a reception 'inverter' her family had acquired. She was convinced it was the closest her family would ever come to experiencing another country, another way of life. International travel remained illegal throughout the 1980s, the fourth decade of the dictatorial reign of

Enver Hoxha. Each mile of the Balkan nation's borders was enforced with bulbous barbed wire.

'Hoxha was paranoid that any Albanian who travelled abroad could be recruited to become a foreign agent, which would threaten his grip on power,' Demollari says. Paranoia, above all else, characterises the 45-year-rule of Albania's former leader. Even the revered missionary Mother Teresa – canonised as a saint in 2016 – was considered a security threat in her home country by Hoxha. The Catholic nun was barred from returning from India to Albania to visit sick relatives. Others who attempted to emigrate were executed.

Some 6,000 Albanians, from a population averaging just two million, were executed for attempting to flee or challenge the state. A further 70,000 were interned as political prisoners.

Free elections failed to arrive when Hoxha died in 1985, leading Demollari to join fellow students in an anti-communism uprising six years later. What began as a hunger strike motivated by the desire for their former leader's name to be removed from the name of a university culminated in the mobilisation of 100,000 people.

Demollari, a languages student at the university, was part of a movement that went on to topple a 7m (22-foot) high bronze statue of Hoxha. 'We chanted as one: *Ne duam që Shqipëria të jetë si pjesa tjetër e Evropës* [We want Albania to be like the rest of Europe],' Demollari recalls, her eyes lighting up.

The fire continues to burn and Demollari, now in her early fifties, is today playing another prominent role in transforming Albania's self-identity and prospects, the face of a unique museum renovated out of the former headquarters of Hoxha's *Sigurimi* secret police.

The 'House of Leaves' museum, so called because of the foliage sprawling up the building's façade, contains chilling insight into the methods of surveillance, interrogation, torture and faux justice delivered in Albania from the 1940s – when some assert that the Nazi party's Gestapo also had a base here – through until 1991.

'The House of Leaves is part of our history, a mysterious place that people of all ages have been curious to visit,' Demollari explains. 'We want to show not only the house, but how it functioned and how its mechanisms were established.'

> We want to make sure that what happened, for far too many years, isn't allowed to happen again in the future. We want to show how the *Sigurimi's* strategies prevented the liberty of thinking, how they made people think only in one way.

> It's for Albanians, but it's for foreigners also; to show how Albania was, so they can understand better this part of our identity. The history of Albania is different to the rest of Europe: more harsh, more [abuse of] power, more isolated.

The museum was curated and funded by Albania's Ministry of Culture. It follows a mission statement to achieve 'cultural integration' with the European Union. In 2006 the government accepted and passed a resolution from the European Council that the crimes of communism should be held equivalent to the crimes of Nazism. This was the first step towards achieving credibility with EU member states.

Within three years Albania had formerly applied for membership. It had seen the likes of Poland, Czechoslovakia and Hungary secure acceptance – and economic optimism – after a record-breaking enlargement. Albania, which has always been fickle in its alliances, did not want to be left behind. The opening of the House of Leaves ten years later embodies the Eastern European nation's sustained efforts to show it does things differently now – and condemns its past sins.

'We were so isolated and all the propaganda about communism versus capitalism was very powerful,' recalls Demollari. "So were the *Sigurimi*, who intimidated the population through psychological violence and control. We have one room which is dedicated to all the persecuted and executed people, which contains all their names. There is another room which shows the political process.'

Court proceedings involved show trials with testimonies typically recorded by bugging equipment attributed to fake personas. Other rooms showcase the wearable technology used by government informers to spy on suspected critics of Hoxha's PLA Party.

Visitors can also see a torture room where political prisoners were interrogated, a laboratory where international mail was screened for invisible ink, and the offices where translators used to transcribe audio interceptions from foreign diplomats.

Albania appears to have convinced many member states of the European Council that the Eastern European outpost now recognises democratic standards. It is poised to accelerate the commencement of accession talks between the European Union and Albania.

'We have always been part of Europe, geographically but also spiritually,' says Demollari, again referencing the 1980 TV inverters to emphasise how the outward looking mentality of ordinary Albanians contrasted with their past politicians.

This not to suggest that the country's current politicians and political parties enjoy a stable affinity with the public either, however. Grievances about education funding morphed into huge demonstrations again recently, articulating more long-standing frustrations about endemic corruption and cronyism in day-to-day living.

Some students are angry about peers being able to buy better grades. Others are angry at the prospect of missing out on jobs to rivals from richer families, who they say will bribe their way into employment.

Sara Kureta, a 19-year-old philosophy undergraduate, told me she believes the prospect of joining the European Union could support her country to move beyond existing as a relatively democratic country, to becoming a truly meritocratic society.

'It's like a culture here to corrupt,' Kureta says. 'Not everyone is corrupt, but people here learn to win things, get things, without working.'

> I don't have much money and my parents don't have rich friends so corruption could be damaging for me. My friend's mother paid to get a job as a nurse, which is really scary to think about, because you shouldn't be able to do a job like that if you aren't qualified to do it.

> To be in the EU you have to have some common values and for us that will be really positive progress. It will be positive for our values and our mentality will change. I see the potential progress in an ethical way, and not in an economic way.

Albania's entry into the European Union remains far from a formality. Recent history has shown us integration can take a decade or more. An alliance of nationalist parties in the European Parliament is currently against further expansion of any kind.

Marsida Turku, a medical student who works in a second museum that commemorates the victims of the Albanian dictatorship, is not discouraged. 'I've been to Italy, Germany and Greece,' she begins. 'Many people in these countries think we are still "in" communism and some that we are in some kind of war.'

'I don't know which war, but they think that we are fighting with another country. I don't know why there is this opinion all over the world, but as a matter of fact we are a democratic country. We are maybe not the most developed country in Europe, but we are trying.'

Turku's museum is carved out of a bunker that Hoxha built for his ministry of defence to work out of, in the unlikely event that nuclear war was declared on his nation.

A time capsule of fear, *BunkArt2* is immersive and amped up with terrifying augmented reality. 'The museum makes more visible how the government used to be before, and how it is now,' the 25-year-old continues.

> We have noticed that lately we are trying hard to reach the level the European Union wants of us. Stopping the corruption is becoming a little bit more aggressive. It is starting to change.

> We are trying to leave a different impression on others. Not only about the corruption, but also to show people that we are focused on other things, like art. We are trying to show the good side of Albania.'

Turku insists however that Albania's fate will not depend on validation from the EU. 'Most young people want to join the Union, but some are in doubt. We've travelled a lot, so we have more differing points of view nowadays. Some of us think it's un-necessary. If we want to do something for our country, we can do so even if we are not part of the European Union.'

The *BunkArt2* guide adds that she has also spent time in Recep Tayyip Erdoğan's Turkey, which ultimately turned its back on the European project to pursue a modern dictatorship of its own. Albania's near-neighbours have jailed around 200,000 political prisoners since giving up on EU assimilation. The freedom to travel abroad has exposed millennial Albanians to a variety of political models. Perhaps there remains cause to be paranoid.

Material from this chapter first appeared on UnHerd *and has been re-published with permission.*

CHAPTER FIFTEEN
RUSSIA – TRAINING AND GAMING

The Sakharov Centre, originally founded by Nobel peace prize winner Andrei Sakharov's widow in 1996, began training ordinary Russians in the realm of 'public defending' back in 2017. It represented a previously little-explored space in the judicial system whereby ordinary Russians can use lawyer privileges themselves to defend or counsel friends and relatives that have either been arrested and detained without charge or face spurious charges against them.

There was surging demand from the off as conventional free legal aid has long been considered by many to be bogus and partisan in favour of the state. The introduction of the Sakharov Centre's public defending service was timely. Hundreds were enduring beating or arrest in 2017 for protesting, as documented by Amnesty International.

When I visited Moscow in the summer of that year, 165 confidants of people detained without charge – or at risk of this – had already signed up to the Centre's new workshops. At these sessions, attendees were informed of the avenues they can follow to get access to the police station or prison where their contact is detained, what documents are needed, and how they can appeal against detentions, treatment and conditions. As a public defender, you have virtually the same rights as a defence lawyer, with the biggest privilege being the almost 24/7 right to visit the cell, the Centre claim.

Its courses in public defending swiftly became 'one of our biggest education projects, though we're not allowed to call our services educational,' Polina Fillipova, who has led the Centre's efforts to raise awareness of the course's availability among young Muscovites, told me at the time. 'To describe yourself as an education provider you need to be registered by the ministry of education and you can be fined and prosecuted if you're caught providing unlicensed education. To get around this we have to describe our programmes as "informational enlightenment" rather than education.'

When Fillipova drily joked 'We've been checked once and thankfully they didn't find any traces of education on us,' it revealed the growing sense of confidence within Moscow's various upstart organisations. Five years ahead of the expanded war in Ukraine, and the tightening censorship that came with it, Russian civil society was beginning to feel they had the means to hold off the state's efforts to silence them.

It hadn't been easy. When the Kremlin passed its 'foreign agents' legislation in 2012 there were fears it could be the end for dissenting voices in Russia. The law banned all political groups funded by non-governmental sources [i.e. all political groups that weren't serving to prop up the regime] from operating unless they applied for a new licence. Notwithstanding the fact that most groups concerned with liberty instantly recognised that any such licences were highly unlikely to be issued to them, few were willing or able to invest the time, money and manpower required to complete the deliberately burdensome paperwork, endless to the point of former Soviet cliché.

The Sakharov Centre fell into this category. 'We didn't do it,' says Fillipova. 'We are an understaffed team and in the time it would have taken us to have attempted that process we could have created and delivered two new courses. The only two organisations in the whole country to comply were two groups in the south of Russia and they only did it to show they were not afraid of the government.'

The government soon came calling on the Sakharov Centre. It fined them 300,000 roubles (£4,000), far more than they had in their reserves. At their annual birthday event in memory of their late founder they managed to raise the funds from their supporters. They were then hit again with a bigger fine. 400,000 roubles this time, for not labelling themselves as foreign agents on their website, or 'wearing the yellow star' as local NGOs have taken to calling it, a reference to persecution seen during the Second World War.

The Centre had no choice but to turn to their loyal supporters again. 'We were worried that people would be offended if we asked for money a second time, but we just thought we *have* to ask. If we don't get the money, so be it, we'll have to close down. That would just mean that it's not what people need at the moment. But we did it. We appealed through our Facebook page this time and raised the money in one month and one day. It still feels great, like a miracle.'

The Centre have had their battles on social media too. 'When we do Facebook advertising, we receive a lot of negative comments from accounts that don't have anything on them, suspiciously empty-looking accounts. Accounts that have been created just to make one post. I wouldn't say there's a state budget for writing shit about Sakharov Centre for five hours a day, but sometimes when we hit the spot, on a crucial social issue, we get social media attacks of that kind.' The existence of so-called troll farms supporting the Kremlin have been exposed by media outlets including BuzzFeed and Radio Liberty.

The human rights hub have won most of their brushes with authority, but at the time of my visit there had been a particularly large shadow hanging over their future. A photo competition their exhibition space held in 2016 featured a picture of Ukrainian soldiers in action in the disputed, occupied territory of Crimea. 'To us it was very clearly a picture illustrating an anti-war message, but to the state duma who wrote to us it represented pro-Ukrainian propaganda. An investigation began into incitement of religious hatred.'

The verdict was yet to reach the Centre when Russia launched its 'special operation' in Ukraine in 2022. The staff fled first to central Europe and on to Western Europe, where the Centre now delivers education, debate, news, analysis and training via radio, website and Telegram platforms.

'Sakharov Radio' is funded by investigative journalism grant-makers Correctiv, Germany's first medium to employ a donation-based model to finance outputs that trigger public debates. Like Sakharov, Correctiv work with citizens on their research, and support society with their educational programmes.

The training in human rights the Sakharov Centre brought to ordinary Russians was complemented prior to the war by a computer game called Gebnya – it translates as 'Bloody KGB' – that left a valuable ongoing legacy through instilling similar legal aware-ness to protect individuals from state-sponsored persecution.

Gebnya gamers navigated a not-so-virtual world in which the central character had to stay one step ahead of state 'tricks' to bring him down (puppet judges, mercenary police and the like). The game was the brainchild of Team 29, a multimedia platform of journalists and lawyers who were keen to foster a sense of resil-ience in their readers by laughing at the 'bully' state machine.

In St Petersburg, where Team 29 was based prior to the 'special operation', anti-government protesters were regularly forced to serve 'administrative arrest' for up to five days in cells with no bedding, according to Amnesty, who described the pre-election crackdowns as 'purposeful humiliation'.

In Soviet times, so-called 'enemies-of-the-state' could be sent to labour camps or executed. Things may briefly have improved in relative terms, but society remains unfree. The work of Team 29 and the Sakharov Centre at least means a far greater number of Russians are these days aware of their rights to express them-selves and the right to support any political movement. Both were enshrined in the 1991 constitution, established when the Russian Federation was born. Article 29, which provides for the right to freely look for, receive, transmit, produce and distribute informa-tion, inspired Team 29's name. Team 29, like the Sakharov Centre, have left Russia now. But the lessons delivered have not.

Material from this chapter first appeared in New Internationalist *and is re-published with permission.*

PART SEVEN

UNCENSOR ME: IMMERSING, SUBVERTING

CHAPTER SIXTEEN

UKRAINE: FORESEEN AND FIGHTING BACK – DYSTOPIAN VISIONING FROM BELARUS

'My heart bleeds for Ukraine and its people,' a Russian friend told me, 'but there is very little those of us with dual citizenships can do without calling a potential court-martial on ourselves. Those in Russia can do even less as their perils are immediate unless the masses rise as they did in the '90s.'

A Ukrainian journalist, Galyna Sergeyeva, has seen such an uprising play out first-hand. 'We Ukrainians proved that everything can be changed if you want it,' the Finland-based news writer says, pointing to her country's Dignity Revolution, staged successfully in 2014, when a corrupt government and wider kleptocracy was brought down.

'I have Russian friends who have been arrested for protesting, but there are too few of them.' On the day we speak, the Russian state-backed broadcaster RT – formerly known as *Russia Today* – has been blocked in Europe. For weeks, RT amplified the Kremlin's line that the Russian government launched its full scale invasion to protect individuals suffering in the east of the country, claiming precision attacks would only hit military targets.

'We have Russian TV in Ukraine, though fortunately less and less,' Sergeyeva continues. 'Russian media is very powerful – and Russian education is also a form of propaganda – but even here in Helsinki, hardly any Russians are vocal against the war. The second-generation Russians here have always had access to independent Russian-language media [and so] they are not zombies. It seems they just don't want to do anything that could compromise themselves.'

Sergeyeva has cousins in Russia and family ties are being tested to the limit by the conflict. 'There are still so many connections. But I am getting more and more convinced that we are totally different now.'

One Russian dissenter described the situation on social media as 'resembling 9/11, only it's your own country that are the terrorists and there are not enough people at the rear of the plane fighting back.'

Belarusian human rights activist Natalia Koliada fears Russian society may have missed its opportunity to decisively push back domestically against propaganda, censorship, and accompanying foreign policy, though Ukraine and its allies have not.

In Belarus in 2020, the presenters, producers and camera operators on state television all left their positions in protest at the scale of murder and rape committed on democracy activists in police cells.

They knew what was happening after the elections and that it was not being reported and so they resigned. What happened? Our dictator, Alexander Lukashenko, brought RT to Minsk and simply replaced everyone who had left.

In Belarus we had our chance to block major propaganda over 26 years [before the electoral violence of 2020], when the names of critics were being erased through dictatorship. It is too easy to say that Russian society is being controlled. It has allowed itself to be controlled. I'm glad to see some people in Russian media now speak out against the war, but why couldn't they have done it when it could have been preventative?

We are speaking in 2022. 'If people in Russia have known for eight years that its government invaded Ukraine eight years ago, and it has continued to live the life it has lived until it became a "wake up call" now, clearly it means there is no society.'

Those going to protests are performing courageous acts and I can only applaud the courage of those people. But this is out of a population of 140 million, so [the small size of protests] means the population is happy. All the major voices are in jail. The population allowed itself to completely lose the idea of freedom and completely accept the bloody regime.

Didn't they have internet all these years? It's only started to switch off now. Did they not use TikTok for video bloggers to talk about luxury bags and cars? Instead of that, it was necessary to scream and shout, to wake up their population.

Journalists and other creatives that can escape Russia ultimately began doing so in huge numbers. Many knew of the purges of their parents' generation and began regrouping in central Asia, dreaming of destinations like Germany. Or Poland, where Koliada, whose early career was spent advocating for nuclear disarmament, is currently based.

Together with her partner Nikolai Khalezin – a former journalist who saw the three newspapers he edited in Belarus shut down by state censors – Koliada recently produced an ominously prescient play, *Dogs of Europe*. Set in 2049, the story sees swathes of the continent subsumed into a Russian super-state after its citizens eschew reading and rioting, turning a blind eye to the dangers of creeping authoritarianism.

'We started the play because we didn't have any space [to resist], but we had the strong belief that if we went underground, we would find all the space of the world. There remains a window for the vision of 2049 to be avoided, but now it is a tiny one. And it is not down to us any more.'

It's much easier to exist in a 'safe bubble', Koliada warns. 'But then it's very easy for any system to manipulate the situation.'

'When freedoms are taken from people it's necessary to stand up. People think that the next morning they will wake up and it will be fine, but it will not be.'

I attend a performance of her play at London's Barbican Theatre, less than a month after the first bombs have been dropped on Kyiv.

Koliada takes to the stage following the performance, where she is greeted by a standing ovation. She reminds the audience that despite protestations of solidarity from the British government, barely 50 refugees had at that time been allowed into the country. She encouraged Londoners to speak to their MPs, to demand a welcome for refugees and for robust sanctions to be applied 'before bombs come to the UK".

Koliada's voice contributed to a growing chorus on these themes that was heard by UK leaders, in the end.

In the play, the protagonists self-censor themselves to the point that they become able only to express themselves involuntarily, once they are sufficiently intoxicated. Koladia says:

> Under the new Reich of the plot narrative, it is the death penalty for anyone that informs on it. Only when they lose control by getting fully drunk do they do allow themselves to perform their beloved Roma dance.

> This is how we lose our personalities, our real 'us'. We start to cower and we start to pretend that we are part of the Reich. And it is when that moment happens that we discover that there is no way out.

> Now, only now, Russia has started to go into the darkest time. Hundreds of politicians are signing letters in support of war, major national theatres are signing letters in support of war – that's it, the Reich is in control.

> In Belarus we talked about it for 28 years and said 'You must stop those two monsters, Alexander Lukashenko and Vladimir Putin'. It's hard when everyone comes back to me to say you were right. I was right. It doesn't help any small children who are killed.

> Does it help the five-year-old daughter of our animator who thinks about whether she will ever see her father again? I'm sure she will see him. But it is the responsibility of Russian people and it is the responsibility of world leaders who really failed democracy. They failed democracy in their countries and in doing that they failed to build democracy in Belarus and Ukraine.

The vision of 2049, where Europe collapses into the grip of a dystopian superstate, can still be avoided, Koladia tells me. 'But it's a tiny window of opportunity. It requires all democratic countries to stand up together and make your governments move as soon as possible."

> Ukrainians, with their lives, are allowing the world to think. But there is no time to think any more. The San Francisco 49ers coach had a slogan which was 'don't tell me, show me,' so there is no time to think. It's time to act now. The time of opportunity is now.

> That's why I'm saying it's not about us any more, it's about you, about the corruption that your government is imposing on your democracies.

The effectiveness of the sanctions regime continues to be scrutinised, with loopholes highlighted through the investigations of organisations such as Transparency International. Meanwhile Koladia fears a crackdown on 'the dirty stream of propaganda' in Europe may also have come too late, with the Russian machine too powerful and dictatorship already 'settled in'.

'We read the Kyiv *Independent*, but all our friends in Ukraine – we talk to them all the time – they are the most trusted sources for us. They tell us what's happening on the ground.'

'This is the most scary moment for a creative person, when your work is so relevant.'

CHAPTER SEVENTEEN
STREET ART TRUTHS – STRENGTHENING POST-MEDIA TURKEY

S ubversive street art and a metaphor laden museum are filling the void left by the death of the free press in Turkey.

The brazen murder of Jamal Khashoggi by Saudi assassins in 2019 failed to prompt the Turkish state to reflect upon how it treats its own media. There was a biting chill in the Bosphorus air for the Istanbul funeral of the late journalist. Some were feeling the early onset of winter. Others were feeling the snap of President Recep Tayyip Erdoğan's resolutely authoritarian regime. Local writer Cigdem Mater was detained at dawn that morning. Her crime? Attempting to establish a new media outlet.

A police report said Mater was planning to stir protests through the platform. If an uprising had been her goal, she was picking the wrong medium, in the wrong country, at the wrong time. Turkey's history of multiple coups has produced insecure political leaders. The Turkish Journalists' Association has bravely continued to record and highlight the hundreds of media professionals jailed since the most recent attempted coup in 2016. A preoccupation with monopolising the media long predates Erdoğan and his AK Party, founded at the turn of the millennium. Only in recent years, however, has the country's free press finally taken its last breaths.

The sale of liberal title *Hürriyet* to new publishers represented the fatal blow. Long-time owners the Dogan Group made the sale reluctantly, ground down by contentious state fines and prosecutions. Hounded for the best part of a decade, the company accrued some 3 billion dollars in penalties. Both the executive publisher and editor-in-chief were jailed. They finally gave up the fight following a constitutional referendum that gave the Dogans no prospect of a reprieve: voters gave Erdoğan a mandate to rule by decree and to remain in post as president until 2034, ending term limits.

With 21 of 29 media brands now overtly backing the ruling party, polling confirms that Turkish readers have given up on the traditional media. The highest level of exposure to 'stories that are completely made up for political or commercial reasons' is reported here. The country came top in a global survey of 74,000 news consumers across 37 countries.

The research was conducted by the Reuters Institute for the Study of Journalism. It found that Turkish readers also held, at the time of the research in 2019, the highest levels of concern that openly expressing their political views online could get them in trouble with authorities. Thought crimes have always been readily penalised here but since public protests in 2013, hundreds of thousands of dissenters have faced jail time, as covered earlier in this book.

I have reportedly on a variety of themes in Turkey and seen that self-censorship is more pervasive here than anywhere else I have worked, from Russia to Ethiopia.

When the constitutional referendum went Erdoğan's way, opposition parties attributed the result to a disparity in access to media coverage. Voters would not support a leader who was imprisoning his own people in such numbers if they were kept informed of the scale of his crackdown, they said. Supporters counter that Erdoğan has earned his many electoral successes, hard-won through reviving the economy [until recently] and advocating traditional, Anatolian values.

How to arrive upon the truth without an independent media to arbitrate? One man is stealthily taking it upon himself to fill the vacuum created by the collapse of critical media. He operates anonymously, nocturnally. 'I want to awaken what each individual lives in their day-to-day lives in Turkey,' says 'Adekan'. The street artist wants Turks to reject the status quo and pursue greater freedoms.

Through spray paints and acrylics, this son of a railway worker depicts sinners and sufferers on urban walls left unguarded at night. The menacing faces he's drawn – some human, some animal, some hybrid monsters – pockmark Istanbul. He says he doesn't assume people will see the same things he sees in the faces he creates, but some almost explicitly evoke political stooges, while others seem sure to conjure up a universal sense of sad powerlessness. Then there are his 'pig portraits'. No-one can look at these pigs without feeling the need to take a shower.

'I expect people feel fear, when they see his work,' a fellow street artist, 'Petuk', tells me as we peer at an image of one of Adekan's most famous faces. It's devil-red and carries the word 'destiny' emblazoned on the forehead. Fear perhaps, but appreciation too. The owner of the building façade invited the pair in for Turkish tea after catching them in the act, we're told.

Others have implored Adekan to draw 'nice things' instead. 'That response makes me angry,' says Adekan. He's studying fine art at university at the time we meet, but his tag name means blood. 'I draw to recoil people. So many people watch television without using their brain. But when they are on the street, I want to splash my art in their eyes. The government uses the media; we use the street. The government is controlling [but] everyone comes to the streets.'

Istanbul's eastern district of Kadikoy has voted against Erdoğan in every election, local or national, since Adekan began practising his craft in the area after relocating from a grey 'closed-minded' industrial city in central Anatolia. His work, along with designs and poetry penned by others galvanised by 'Gezi' five years ago [an environmental campaign at Gezi Park that morphed into a mega civil rights protest] now appears all over Turkey's former capital.

Adekan is clear that the rise in creative protest has come out of necessity. It has been born out of strict censorship, police brutality and bogus prosecutions. It must not be romanticised. 'There is a heightened consciousness at the moment but it will only be important if [expression] can continue,' he says. 'It is not safe to speak out. It is always difficult to predict how people will react.'

Kadikoy is Istanbul's most tolerant quarter. The municipality has sponsored an international street art festival each year since the Gezi protests. Nonetheless, our voices hush as a police officer walks into the café we're meeting in, at the ferry port on the Asian shore of the Bosphorus. We silently move on, in much the same way reporters are quietly censoring themselves across Turkey every day now.

Orhan Pamuk, Turkey's most famous journalist, is among those now practising self-censorship. The Nobel prize winning author simply can't practise journalism in Istanbul, the city that made him, without provoking charges of 'Insulting Turkishness' and the accompanying prison sentences they bring.

A 20-minute boat ride away, on the European side of the city, he has curated some protest art of his own. The Museum of Innocence, a three-storey private museum based on his book of the same name, is a unique portrait of Istanbul, his life and the struggle to speak uncomfortable truths in climates of fear. It centres on the story of a fictional journalist who hoarded objects from an illegitimate love's house during a previous post-coup crackdown.

'Disparate objects, when placed side by side, can bring forth unprecedented thoughts and emotions,' is the concept's claim. Like Adekan, Pamuk has found a means to swerve censorship in an attempt to safeguard Turkish society from losing sight of the repressions being committed, without conventional accountability, in its post-media age.

'Just how dangerous is it to work as a journalist in Istanbul?', I ask the museum supervisor. He's too cowed to discuss it, but he scribbles the name Hrant Dink on a post-it note. Dink was a Turkish-Armenian journalist, assassinated in 2007 for narrating Turkey's denial of the Armenian genocide a century ago. A photo later surfaced of Dink's killer, flanked by smiling Turkish police, posing in front of the Turkish flag. As Istanbul and the wider world continues to mourn Khashoggi, so it should mourn the wider death of journalism here. Street artists need shadows to work in, but these are long shadows indeed.

Material from this chapter first appeared in openDemocracy *and is re-published with permission.*

PART EIGHT

TECH CONTROL: DIGITAL DYNAMITE

CHAPTER EIGHTEEN

HACKTIVISM HOLD-OUTS –
AUDACIOUS CODING INSPIRES
IRANIAN PROTESTS

'Hacktivism' entails the use of hacking and digital technology to promote a political or social cause. Hacktivists use their technical skills to hack into computer systems, websites, or social media accounts to spread their message, disrupt the normal operation of targeted systems, or steal and leak sensitive information.

Sergey Shykevich is Cyber Threat Intelligence Manager at Check Point Security. Vocationally, it is something of an asset for cyber security professionals to possess, or at least adopt, a paranoid and pessimistic temperament when it comes to keeping a step ahead of hactivists.

'It may be too soon to refer to hacktivism as state-sponsored terrorism, but there is no doubt that it is becoming harder to disconnect one from the other,' Shykevich says gloomily. 'As geopolitical tensions continue to dominate the world agenda this new age of cyberwarfare will only get worse, before it gets better.'

However, while coding itself may be binary, those who work with it are not. 'Hactivism can be an effective way to bring attention to a cause, raise awareness, and hold powerful organisations or governments accountable,' Shykevich acknowledges. 'Hacktivists can use their skills to expose corruption, human rights abuses, or other injustices that might not otherwise be brought to light. They can also disrupt the operations of organisations or governments they see as harmful or oppressive.'

He himself is not averse to disruptive tactics. I learn this through his movements in the planning stages of our interview as much as from the answers he ultimately provides to my questions. Our appointment in Tel Aviv was initially postponed because Shykevich joined others in the Israeli tech community in striking during the rule of law protests that engulfed the country in early 2023. The industrial action and peaceful protests Shykevich took part in proved decisive – as we shall explore in a later chapter – in securing delays and concessions from a government that had previously appeared intent on rushing through controversial judicial reforms.

I had been intrigued to meet Shykevich since stumbling across his research into the subversive successes of an audacious hactivist group prominent in Iran named Predatory Sparrow. Shykevich's research study homed in on cyberattacks conducted by Predatory Sparrow against Iran's state broadcaster in the run up to the 2022 Mahsa Amini uprising.

At the time of writing almost 20,000 Iranians had been arrested for daring to take part in the Mahsa Amini protests, this after the 22-year-old woman they were defending had died in police custody. She had been detained by morality police for allegedly not wearing her hijab properly. The protests have been described as the biggest threat to the Iranian regime since the Islamic Revolution in 1979.

In addition to demands for increased rights for women, the protests have demanded the overthrow of the Islamic Republic, taking demands a fearless step further than previous major protest movements in Iran, including that seen in 2019 when 1,500 people were killed.

Predatory Sparrow first asserted their influence with a hack in July 2021 targeted at the country's train station schedule boards. A message projected onto platform monitors referred perplexed passengers to the Supreme Leader's office phone number.

Three months later, each and every petrol station in Iran was paralysed by an attack that disrupted the electronic payment process system. The incident led to extremely long queues for two days and prevented customers from paying with the government-issued electronic cards used to purchase subsidised fuel. When the card was swiped for payment, the Supreme Leader's office phone number appeared once more on the screens. The highest ranking office of the regime was being taunted a second time.

The tactics went largely unreported outside of the country until Check Point published its investigation into the group's follow-up assault on Iran's state broadcaster. In January 2022, several state-run TV channels found themselves broadcasting footage of opposition leaders (following another hack). The web-based streaming platform of the state broadcaster was hijacked days later, presenting protest messages urging citizens to rise up against the Supreme Leader and stating that 'the regime's foundations are rattling'. The incident took place in the middle of a live broadcast of the Iran-UAE soccer match, described as a 'clever' ploy in Check Point's research report.

Predatory Sparrow have called for the assassination of Iran's Supreme Leader and Shykevich describes some of their tactics, which he links backs to Syria-based anti-regime outfit Indra, as unethical and illegal'.

'Overall, the Check Point report suggests that Predatory Sparrow and Indra were motivated by a desire to expose what they saw as social and political injustices and to hold powerful organisations and governments accountable for their actions.'

Iran's protests remained live and ongoing as this book was being finalised in the autumn of 2023. But Shykevich was happy to point to several hactivist movements that have already delivered on their objectives. Hacks deemed impactful highlighted by Shykevich included #OpJusticeForGeorgeFloyd. This hack exposed police brutality in the US ahead of the conviction of disgraced officer Derek Chauvin.

'While hacktivism is not without controversy and may involve illegal or unethical actions, it has been successful in achieving some of the goals of certain individuals and groups.'

Maureen Webb, a constitutional lawyer, documents a range of global impacts in her book *Coding Democracy – How Hackers Are Disrupting Power, Surveillance and Authoritarianism*. Much of her research took place in Germany, where the hacker ethos of 'transparency for the powerful and privacy for the weak' has always run deepest.

'Graffiti artists and hackers moved into East Berlin at the same time and they had a lot of similar ideas about reclaiming space,' Webb explains. 'A lot of the ideas behind graffiti, philosophical ones, were similar to those that the Chaos Computer Club was talking about at the time.'

The Chaos Computer Club is Europe's largest association of hackers, formed after the fall of the Berlin Wall and the invention of the internet in the early 1990s. An international forum has convened in the German capital every four years for the past three decades, making the country the epicentre of transgressive innovation in cyberspace.

'Hackers have translated the Enlightenment's ideas of liberty, fraternity and equality for the digital age, with principles like privacy and transparency, as well as their striving for data self-determination, anti-monopolisation and net neutrality.'

Webb's book reflects that it was in Germany that hackers first 'saved democracy' by identifying flaws in electronic voting systems, with coders demonstrating how they could manipulate the counters to play chess against one another rather than process polling tallies. The Netherlands subsequently banned the electronic voting technology as too risky.

Germany also saw the policies of its interior minister challenged by hackers who successfully captured the official's fingerprints, reproducing them in gelatin for citizens to wear within facsimile gloves as they passed through security desks. It exploded the perception that biometric passports, those using fingerprints, were less susceptible to fraud than traditional passports. It was also, Webb recalls, 'hilarious'.

'The Chaos Computer Club has become increasingly like a friend of the court, or a valued witness in government committees, looking at the introduction of biometric technologies and the particular dangers of it.'

Vulnerabilities in vaccine passport technology have more recently been highlighted by hactivists in Webb's native Canada. 'One group hacked the QR codes of several prominent politicians and another group successfully created false proof of vaccination for non-existent people and registered them in the apps within hours. It showed this kind of centralised collection of information is extremely dangerous and the more you link it with other databases, the more dangerous it becomes.'

'These systems, when combined with artificial intelligence (AI), the power of them is unimaginable compared to the systems we were using ten years ago.' Webb believes society is entering a technology 'arms race' where hackers face a disadvantage in terms of the data they have access to, but have a vital role to play in highlighting threats to individual liberty.

The author lectures at Boston's MIT university, with some of her recent research exploring the implications of Chinese-style benefit systems, which have recently migrated as far afield as Brazil, that can be combined with centrally-controlled digital currency. 'The state can access the power to turn your currency on and off, like its more like a token of entitlement than an [authentic] currency that people can use freely.'

'These emerging digital systems will not only change our societies, they threaten to destroy our democracies and also to destroy our humanity because if you really follow developments in AI and transhumanism, there are some changes coming at us that only people who read science fiction had any idea might be possible within this century.'

In terms of how governments respond to resistance from hackers, Webb says the current global trend points towards 'ruthless intolerance' of hackers interrogating digital systems, despite the vital role their 'technical brilliance and creativity' can play in preserving democratic principles. And the intolerance is from governments that identify themselves as liberal as much as it is from regimes such as those in Iran or Belarus, where the government is currently fighting a physically militarised hacktivism opposition.

'My concern when I wrote the book was really more about right-wing authoritarianism, surveillance and situations of power, that the right-wing had facilitated in the George W Bush era. What I'm more concerned about now are the technocratic solutions that left and liberal governments are bringing to bear to exert social control and to grab and retain power.'

Naomi Colvin is a Director at the European NGO Blueprint for Free Speech. There she has observed similar patterns to Webb in the decade since Wikileaks disrupted the prevailing world order with its exposing of the US espionage of private citizen communication. Colvin previously led the Courage Foundation, co-founded by Julian Assange of Wikileaks, to support whistleblowers and journalists through fundraising for their legal defence.

> There was a popular groundswell about that time around defending free expression; common decency against the machine. Then a fork in the road was taken, where a lot of the people who were doing really creative and idealistic things in this medium were basically prosecuted by the US – arrested or put out of action in various ways. There is a link between that and the sort of more nihilistic stuff that came up after it, once the idealistic people were taken out of the system.
>
> There is still an important role for hacktivists to play. Belarus is really interesting, because there you have hacktivists who have joined forces with trade unionists and others to do civil society protests. This pre-dates Russia's invasions of Ukraine. However the sentence for designing sabotage in Belarus is the death penalty.'

Spain, sometime painted as the 'paradise for guerilla communications' has realised many media-genic milestones. Barcelona-based Xnet have brought corrupt bankers to justice after pensions were ransacked. Phineas Fisher brought high-profile scrutiny to Catalan police after a YouTube video illuminating the revolutionary's hacktivism tactics turned the tables on officers suspected of framing a suspect.

'The future of hacktivism and whistleblowing is connected,' Colvin argues. 'In practice a lot of this activism can be mediated through journalists, rather than through dramatic and showy spectacles which happen online.

> I'm involved in a lot of discussions in Europe where we're seeing increasingly creative use of the legal system to harass journalists or harass activists. We're seeing those with computer networks being charged with computer crimes, and also countries with wealthy individuals filing criminal complaints to do with GDPR [data protection legislation] or criminal defamation suits to harass journalists.

> Countering these threats is always a moving target. I was going to say that the penalties involved for hacktivism are higher than for on the ground activism, but maybe that's evening out in the UK with the new [Public Order Act] legislation. The bill, recently passed as law, stands to remove freedoms for individuals once they have attended a second peaceful protest.

> A lot of our conversations in Europe are with Polish defence lawyers, who have a lot of experience defending activists that have been hit by misdemeanour offences, merely for turning up at protests.

With suppression suffocating disparate societies, minds may wander back to Mahsa Amini in Iran. And indeed Sergey Shykevich in Israel and how our initial interview was postponed so he could take part in peaceful protest action. It's easy to imagine which path coders may turn to if rights to free speech are more widely removed. The same software skills can be used to challenge as well as to uphold systems of control.

CHAPTER NINETEEN

NETWORKING FOR PRIVACY –
ETHIOPIA'S INTERNET TRIUMPHS

Tigrayans, an ethnic group representing just six per cent of Ethiopia's population, 'own' the country's coalition government. This was the view of the Ethiopian Border Affairs Committee NGO in 2017. And it fairly reflected the resentment felt by much of the majority ethnic group, the Oromo people, towards the ruling elite.

The lack of representation felt by the Oromia region, which is made up mostly of Oromo people and contains Ethiopia's capital Addis Ababa, had fuelled a series of protests prior to my visiting that year. I wanted to see how reactive restrictions on free expression, association, and peaceful assembly, described as draconian by Human Rights Watch, were impacting resistance.

A seesaw battle for control of – and access to – the internet was playing out at the time, the first major cyber battle of this kind to be fought in Africa. The internet war was largely being waged between the ruling regime, led by the Tigrayan People's Liberation

Front Party, and a new generation of software-smart young professionals in Addis Ababa.

While there have been policies restricting access to the internet across the world, they had arguably never been attempted on the scale seen in Ethiopia. The country has 100 million people but utilised only one internet server provider, owned by the government. A state of emergency directive approved in October 2016 placed heavy restrictions on the use of social media and other online communication.

'It was completely shut down two days before the state of emergency was declared,' recalls 27-year-old Abraham, a web developer at a digital marketing start-up. 'Over time, access to email sites became available, for people who have access to WiFi. Most people in Addis, let alone the rest of Ethiopia, don't have access to WiFi. Every other website was blocked.'

One week after the state of emergency was called, any internet communication that could be taken to 'create misunderstanding between people' was made illegal. The government was most concerned by Facebook, through which it said videos of arson were being posted by protesters to inspire copycat attacks. Activists also posted videos of police and security forces assaulting Oroma rebels. Five-year prison sentences became the deterrent for publishing such material, but for most even basic access to the internet became impossible.

But the Oromia region's new generation of graduates stepped forward to show that the country's majority group – wholly unrepresented in parliament at the time – had the digital skills to win the communication wars of the future.

'The circle of developers in Addis is small, but we all talk and so we were quick to establish the VPNs (virtual private networks) that would enable us to access data as soon as it was first blocked,"'explains Abraham from his office in downtown Addis.

Phone communication was also blocked at the time, but developers and others who knew how to get around the shutdown asked around until they found a contact that had both an unblocked VPN app and an app sharing device that did not rely on an internet connection.

'The government fought back, switching off the ports connecting the unsecured VPNs to the internet,' Abraham continues in hushed tones, 'but we then found others that were still connected, and so on until eventually the government decided just to unblock the internet again, for Addis at least, two weeks ago.' We're speaking in January 2017, while the government's state of emergency is still in place. 'Although access to social media is still technically blocked, the government no longer seem to be attempting to disconnect VPNs.'

In the capital, the government seem to have admitted defeat in their attempts to mute the citizens most determined to get online. Abraham, when I spoke to him, appears to have found the battle an amusing intellectual challenge rather than a political crusade. 'One should not be denied his right to free internet,' he joked, adopting a grand intonation.

Abraham's compatriots have found the government's repressive tactics anything but amusing, however. It was clear in 2017 that should apps like Super VPN and Xender – a tool that enables people to share and open VPN apps even if they are not logged on – make their way from Addis to southern Oromia, they would be greeted as political tools rather than technological novelties, and Prime Minister Hailemariam Desalegn would feel the heat rise.

Toler, a 25-year-old graduate juggling two jobs, told me he believed the government's digital policy had allowed it to cling on to power in the short term. However, he anticipated the censorship's financial impact would ultimately be more devastating than the protests had been.

'Our economy is very small,' he said. 'People focus on the growth, but we have a tiny economy, in its infancy. The internet policy meant Ethiopia only performed to 20 per cent of our capacity in the last two months. Forty per cent of our exports will directly go towards paying off our debts.'

Toler was well placed to evaluate the cost. In his day job he was working as an economist at one of the country's leading banks, able to connect to WiFi transmitted by the hotel adjacent to his office.

He showed me a PDF on his Samsung Galaxy of World Bank statistics emphasising the debt Ethiopia is in to China.

'From an economic view, I don't know how we're going to get out of this,' he said. 'For the economy to change, the politics has to change. The "development state" – growth first, human rights later – this ideology has to change. I'm very scared for the future of our country, all of us are.'

Toler was trying to grow a fashion chain in his spare time and claimed to have lost up to 200,000 Birr ($8,780) in revenue due to the internet restrictions. 'I'm relatively better educated than an average Ethiopian and I know how to use these technologies like VPNs. Imagine what the policy has meant to the average person who runs a business and doesn't know how to use all this complicated stuff. Ethiopians have got used to relying on WhatsApp and Viber to discuss prices and that sort of thing, but most haven't been able to access these apps since the block.'

With people like Abraham and Toler spreading awareness of apps like Super VPN, which allows users to browse the internet without any restrictions, the unanswered question during my visit was whether the return of social media will see it harnessed to challenge Tigrayan rule again.

'A lot of people care about the nationality (ethnicity)', says Toler, 'but I don't care what the backgrounds of our politicians are, as long as they have the mindset to change our country.'

'For all the weaknesses Ethiopia has, we also have enormous opportunities as a country. We cannot allow the economy to be disrupted by internet shutdowns. 'We have a population of 100 million people. You can sell anything to 100 million people.'

One year later, Oromo upstart Abiy Ahmed swept to power, destroying the Tigrayan-led coalition at the ballot box after the internet crackdown proved futile.

After initially receiving global acclaim and a Nobel peace prize for bridging divides between Oromos and Tigrayans, Ethiopia ultimately descended into civil war. This came after a new power struggle broke out between the Tigrayan People's Liberation Front and Prime Minister Abiy, who went on to impose communication blackouts of his own amid a ruthless arms bombardment of Tigray.

Ethiopia's digital communication battleground reminds us that the tech savvy of resistance movements can become tools of repression when commitment to peaceful governance is dispensed with by leaders who feel threatened.

Ethiopia's internal war with Tigray lasted almost two years, with the communication black-outs ensuring the full scale and nature of the conflict remained difficult to verify throughout the most horrific of conflicts. The fragile peace agreement brokered appears to lack routes to reparative justice for the victims of crimes obscured by internet shutdowns.

Prime Minister Abiy Ahmed was celebrated too soon as a saviour. Similarly, no prizes should be given out prematurely for software sophistication itself, when it can swiftly be redeployed for silencing survivors as much as it can sometimes play a role in safeguarding the vulnerable.

Material from this chapter first appeared in New Internationalist *and is re-published with permission.*

PART NINE

OUTSIDE > IN: ESCAPE AND OPPORTUNISM

CHAPTER TWENTY
REIMAGINING CRISIS RESPONSE – REFUGEES WANTED

The mythical gladiators of ancient Rome are glorified in our collective imaginations. In truth, those who died for the entertainment of privileged voyeurs were predominantly prisoners of past wars in Ethiopia, condemned outcasts, or others considered undeserving of legal protection.

The 'spectacle' of unwitting combat, replete with ancient power imbalances, returned to Italy in the 2010s alongside the rise of populism embodied by former interior minister Matteo Salvini. It has continued under current Prime Minister Giorgia Meloni. The arena, once the Colosseum, is now the streets, squats and makeshift refugee camps of Rome.

Travel six stops north of the Colosseum on Metro Line B and witness how an Italy re-made by Salvini, Italy's most influential politician even in the periods when he's not serving as an MP, has evoked the harsh, domineering spirit of the empire.

The sprawling Tiburtina station concourse forms the benign backdrop to the most in-demand refugee camp hosted by the

Baobab Experience NGO. Its specific location (to the east or west of the station) varies month to month. This is because the tents, toilets and cooking facilities belonging to Baobab, a voluntary association supporting vulnerable migrants, have been bulldozed dozens of times over.

Social worker Marianna Maggi says refugees have become Italy's 'fake enemies.... They are scared and tell us everyone hates them since Salvini.'

Salvini abolished humanitarian protection for migrants refused refugee status, impacting up to 100,000 individuals. Since seeing his law passed, Salvini set about creating as big a spectacle as possible in 'cleaning the streets', the mantra during his pre-election campaigning.

Photos of his 'gladiator heroes' – and their fearful targets – perform well with Salvini's millions of social media followers. So do the images of demolished shelters.

Baobab told me in 2019 that some 70,000 migrants had received support with legal and healthcare challenges from the organisation over the preceding four years. But their Tiburtina site has become as brittle as the states its beneficiaries have travelled from, countries such as Sudan and Eritrea.

'Public opinion strongly appreciated Salvini's approach,' according to Giovanna De Maio, a former resident or Rome who now works as a foreign policy analyst at the Brookings Institution in Washington. 'Security and economic prosperity are two areas Italians have been feeling particularly vulnerable about for at least a decade.'

'We are left to live like animals – this is no life,' says one, sleeping in a disused former Tor Vergata University building in the south-eastern suburbs. At the time we speak, Rome had recently recorded up to 11,000 individuals making do in abandoned factories, office buildings and other properties. Salvini introduced four-year prison sentences for anyone thinking of joining them, without providing alternatives.

Another migrant, who had been relying on the Baobab camp, now planned to try his luck in Barcelona. 'They don't allow people to live on the streets there,' he says. Such testimonies bring dark cheers from many in Italy, who elected Georgia Meloni of the neo-fascist Brothers of Italy party as their prime minister in 2022.

'The politicians are following the sentiment of the people,' says Alessandro Falcioni, who works for a Catholic charity supporting refugees. 'The stomach is punctured here.'

Falcioni says Europe must accept some blame for not providing more solidarity during the peak period of boat migration in 2015. Falcioni's organisation, *Cittadini del Mondo* (Citizens of the World), has established an 'intercultural library' in efforts to promote greater understanding across communities.

The multilingual *biblioteca* was designed to organically bring communities together, while there is a help desk in place on site that provides migrants with a virtual fixed address. This detail empowers individuals to apply for work permits.

'With our work we pursue another view, another way,' says Falcioni. Both refugees and host countries need charities like this, but increasingly the organisations themselves are now being persecuted.

The Greek government, for example, has upset local refugee NGOs by accusing them of fronting human trafficking operations. A fresh department serving the re-elected New Democracy party has been established that can revoke, at will, the registrations of organisations representing vulnerable migrants.

'The registration procedure is just another part of a wider deterrence agenda,' according to Elli Xenou, a senior advocacy worker at the Athens branch of the Doctors of the World charity. Her organisation has been ordered to submit two years' worth of detailed financial accounts in order to maintain its status. The exercise is relatively straightforward for international organisations such as Xenou's. However it is suffocating for threadbare grass roots outfits and physically impossible for start-ups.

The measures have been implemented in parallel with a new International Protection Act. The legislation has pushed vulnerable migrants further to society's margins by reducing residency terms provided to those granted refugee status from three years to one.

'The new asylum law and the defaming and blaming of NGOs... they are all different pieces of the same puzzle that is to make refugees and migrants' lives unbearable so as not to create a pull factor for more to come to Europe,' Xenou continues.

'Ethnocentric policies may add a challenge – a barrier – but you don't put an end to the people's hope for a future, for a better life, for peace this way.'

The state is increasingly reluctant to support asylum seekers with their basic needs. Policies mirror hardening public attitudes. New legislation introduced to Greece gives those granted refugee status just one month to find independent accommodation while the law blocks access to earning an income through paid work for six months. Road maps to shelter, foundations and respite are cynically curtailed.

Meanwhile, Greece's 83 refugee NGOs are consumed with the expensive new auditing requirements imposed upon them, labelled 'discriminatory' in some quarters for not applying to charities working with beneficiaries that are not migrants.

Where people have needed help, a void has been created. Ironically, genuine traffickers have been happy to step in, working the impoverished, urine-soaked Omonia and Victoria Squares of central Athens, homing-in on the disenfranchised.

'The asylum service never asked me one question about my circumstances for leaving Syria,' Yasser tells this writer, when we meet at a detention centre on the Aegean island of Kos. 'All they talked about was my return to Turkey. That's what made me want to escape [Greece].'

The 49-year-old father of seven children subsequently paid a trafficker from north Africa 1,000 Euros for a clandestine ride across the border to Serbia, beginning an uncertain odyssey towards the UK.

Greek officials displayed scant interest in Yasser but counterparts in Europe will likely have shown more concern. All asylum seekers have their own story to tell. Sometimes their past experiences are complex and confounding. This self-described 'scientist-turned-accountant', travelling anonymously and undocumented through the Serbian mountains into the Schengen zone, defies the stock summary of either side of the culture war divisions.

Yasser fled Syria when his house in Damascus was bombed by Israeli jets, he says. He also shares that when living in the capital city, he worked at the infamous Syrian Scientific Studies and Research Centre. An agency of President Bashar al-Assad's dictatorial government, the heavily-bombed facilities have allegedly served as a primary base for the development of nuclear, biological and chemical weapons.

The Syrian government insists the organisation is purely a 'civilian research centre'. Three years ago 217 employees were blacklisted by the US government for the alleged use of sarin gas on civilians.

Greece's migration and asylum minister Notis Mitarachi has accused NGOs based there of squandering 1.3 billion Euros in European Union funding during the refugee crisis. Yet the Greek government itself is the administration primarily tasked, along with that in Turkey, of processing the asylum claims of irregular migrants entering Europe.

The Greek Council for Refugees is one of many NGOs to argue that politicians across multiple borders have failed to deliver during the refugee crisis, which first emerged and peaked in 2016 and is now bubbling again. 'It has not been a *refugee* crisis,' says spokesperson Spyros Oikonomou, 'it has been a *management* crisis.'

'The years immediately after 2016 were really not that challenging. We are talking about roughly 120,000 people between 2016 and 2020. Divide that by the number of member states and see how easy it would be to resolve it tomorrow.'

'My humble opinion is that this could have been avoided if from the very beginning we had had a proper distribution mechanism, for every country to just get a fair proportion [of asylum claims] and for everyone to be able to move forward in a more humane and legitimate manner.'

Not all political blocs act as the European Union is currently. The East African Community (EAC), a growing economic coalition of countries, is blazing a trail in embracing the benefits that can be brought about by softening borders. Refugees from EAC countries can now claim the rights of citizens in any other nation within the bloc. This includes the freedom of movement and the right to work.

The breakthrough follows a study by the World Bank in 2015 and 2016 which concluded that increased overall average local income and employment in Kenya's Turkana county is attributable to the Kakuma refugee camp established there.

Refugees from EAC countries need to choose to give up their refugee status and the protections and assistance that go with it under the EAC agreement – which is not a small decision – if they choose to take up the citizenship.

However, citizenship brings long-term security and opportunities of a type not afforded to most refugees in Greece, Italy and Kenya. As refugees in East Africa increasingly choose this path instead of encampment, the trend in turn frees up resources to respond to other refugee populations in need of protection and assistance, and host communities see income and employment levels rise. The model in East Africa shows that the benefits of welcoming refugees contrasts sharply with the narratives currently being exploited by populist politicians in Europe.

It is inappropriate and it now been established as unlawful to consider sending asylum seekers in Europe to East Africa, as the British government had planned to do. But European governments may instead do well to look to import or regain a mentality of welcoming and valuing people fleeing war and persecution.

Material from this chapter first appeared in New Internationalist *and is re-published with permission.*

CHAPTER TWENTY-ONE
SPORTING CHANCE: DOORS AJAR

The first mixed gender relay in the history of the world athletics championships was heralded by organisers as a statement of equality and inclusivity. This moment was celebrated when it was integrated into the competition in 2019. It was staged in Qatar, a country synonymous with gendered segregation. However Gulf leaders' love of sport – while they will find no cheerleaders in these pages for their human rights record documented elsewhere in this book – is contributing towards bridging competing social values in the Middle East.

'Inclusion is a big thing and seeing strong women perform is amazing for this region,' the renowned sprinter and women's rights campaigner Alysson Felix told me after steering 'Team USA' to victory in the relay final.

Earlier in the year Felix had secured greater rights for women in America, successfully lobbying her sponsors Nike to end its practice of withholding bonuses to athletes who chose to have children. Now the Californian wants to play her role in realising greater equality and inclusion for women and girls in the Gulf.

She is encouraged by how athletics has already brought changes to the desert nation's metropolis hub in recent years, even before the staging of what, at the time, represented the biggest sporting event ever held in the Middle East.

Athletics' circuit for professional athletes, the Diamond League, has had a presence in Doha every year for more than a decade. Professional athletes who choose to accept invitations have been provided with plenty of opportunities to explore the city – in which the majority of both Qataris and expats live – beyond the confines of the capital's gleaming Khalifa International Stadium.

'Since I've been coming here I've gone into some of the schools and when I first started coming not all the girls were active because of what can be worn,' Felix explains. Most Qataris follow the conservative Salafi interpretation of Islam, also adhered to by the majority of Sunni Muslims in neighbouring Saudi Arabia. The expectation to remain covered has historically made outdoor sports largely inaccessible for girls and women in countries where temperatures can hit 50 degrees.

Things are evolving. Felix, whose victory left her with more world titles to her name than Usain Bolt, has spent time exploring 'Education City', a blossoming 14 square kilometre (5.4 square miles) campus of schools and universities in Doha's northern suburbs funded by the state's ruling Al-Thani monarchy.

Education City features Qatar's first non-segregated schools and international universities where students can wear what they choose. Moreover, there's an array of sports clubs and facilities open to all genders.

Three-quarters of students are women and by all accounts are far higher achievers than their male counterparts. 'I now see so many more [women] involved,' smiles Felix. 'Like anything there's always more [barriers] to go, but I hope we're moving in the right direction, even though sometimes it feels slow.'

The Greek pole vaulter Katerina Stefanidi told me she had observed a shift in the local cultural expectations of women since Qatar started welcoming international stars on an annual basis in 2010. The dress rules enforced in the stadium have been less strict each year she's visited. 'I think Qatar is changing,' she said.

The Gulf region was represented by Bahrain in the mixed relay. The sprinter Salwar Eid Naser, who was permitted to make the personal decision not to wear her hijab during a humid week here in Doha, inspired her team to a surprise bronze medal. 'I'm not doing it for myself alone; I'm doing it for the people who look up to me,' she told reporters, wiping sweat from her brow.

Some athletes suggested that the Qatari organisers and the monarchy are only keen for the desert nation to be seen at its most tolerant and inclusive in the ten days while it has the eyes of the world's media upon it.

The ruling Emir still refuses to allow women the right to pass citizenship rights down to their children if the father is not Qatari, two decades after Egypt scrapped its own patrilineage rules. Females under 25 continue to require the consent of a male relative to travel independently abroad. Saudi Arabia lifted similar restrictions in 2019, leaving Qatar as the only country in the Gulf region still blocking women from flying without authorisation.

The leaders of these neighbouring countries both came to power young, in their thirties, having developed a passion for sport while studying at universities in Yorkshire in the north of England. Both nations have been accused of 'sports-washing', staging sporting events in order to improve their international reputations, when a more prosaic interpretation is that exposure to the contemporary inclusivity of sport has served to begin to modernise regimes.

Patriarchy persists but experiences are more varied than sometimes perceived, according to Reem Meshal, a Professor of Middle Eastern Studies at Education City's Hamed Bin Khalifa University. 'I've encountered women who have never had a problem, that their father or brothers have never stood in the way of their travel or education, and then I've also met others for whom, yes, it's a problem; a priority,' the Egyptian says.

I spoke with a 17-year-old Qatari facing cultural barriers preventing her from exploiting talents for a range of sports, despite perceptions that her country is broadly becoming more inclusive. She does not wish to give her full name for fear of experiencing a 'lot of trouble'"within her family.

Sara said she was approached by Doha's world-renowned Aspire Academy, which trains precocious junior athletes, after showing promise in football, volleyball and swimming in school competitions. 'It's hard to do these sports with a scarf on. My family tell me the gates to heaven will close if I show my hair. If it was in my hands I would go outside Qatar, where people would not care how I dress.'

Stigma impacted her relationships with other girls at school also. 'The students think I have bad intentions if I wear my abaya open,' she says. 'I wear make-up because it makes me feel more confident, but people think badly of me for doing it. If I could change one thing about Qatar it would be the way people see women here.'

Aisha Al-Naama, an athletics fan from Doha, has had better experiences. 'My friends are encouraged to enter marathons now and one even competed in an '"ron woman". You would never have seen that in Qatar ten years ago, when you might have been barred from entering local competitions if you were a Qatari woman.'

The 30-year-old defends her country's customs around guardianship, insisting families rarely impose their will in practice. 'There has to be a family consensus [on international travel] here because we're not an individualistic society, we're a group-based society,' Al-Naama argues. 'It's to do with the social structure here, which promotes the idea of a family, the idea of a group, the idea of co-existing.'

In athletics, the relay competition is unique in creating space for championing the potential of the individual and the collective when they seek greater synergy together. It has long been emblematic, but in Qatar during its world athletics championships, perhaps more than ever.

SECTION TEN - AGENCY GAINED: HOLDING COURT

CHAPTER TWENTY-TWO
AMNESTY OVER – LEBANON BLASTS BACK

In August 2020, the Port of Beirut in Lebanon experienced one of the largest non-nuclear explosions the world has ever seen. The whole country shook, with tremors also felt in Turkey, Syria, Palestine, Jordan and Israel. The blast was even heard in Cyprus, 240km (150 miles) away.

Three years later, still no-one has been held accountable. I seek out Nadim Houry, a lawyer who founded Human Rights Watch in Lebanon and now runs the Arab Reform Initiative, an NGO based in Paris.

'Anyone who cares about change in Lebanon recognises that we have always been held back by the issue of impunity. Even at a young age, growing up in the country, I could see it was always about impunity.'

300,000 people were left homeless in the wake of the Beirut Port blast. More than 200 people were killed, 7,000 were injured and over 15 billion dollars' worth of property was damaged or destroyed.

'The regime has turned out to be more resilient,' explains Houry, who led Human Rights Watch in Lebanon for 13 years after being 'admitted to the bar' – qualifying in law – in New York. He says:

> The response to the port explosion is very telling. The investigative judge pushed and named some high ranking officials. The political class – which often operates this way – recognised that while their interests are divided, their existence was at risk and so they came together. They stood united and blocked the investigation.
>
> The political class continues blocking the investigation from going forwards. They come up with things. They threaten the judge. They create real intimidation.
>
> Two of the former ministers who were charged by the judge refused to appear before him. Then the minister of the interior refused to implement the arrest warrant. The system is rejecting the investigation.
>
> The two wanted ministers went on to run in elections, with one winning again their seat in parliament. Now he is saying he has parliamentary immunity, so the system of impunity has shown that it has quite a high level of resilience."

There is no justice in sight for what Houry says is 'at best criminal negligence': the unsafe six-year storage of more than a kiloton of ammonium nitrate at the port of Lebanon's capital city.

He says the stifling corruption holding Lebanon down can be traced back to an Amnesty Law established in 1991 following the country's 15-year civil war. The move pardoned political crimes committed during the conflict years but as a legacy, attempts have often been made since then to brush contemporary sins under the carpet.

'The problems in Lebanon are a manifestation of a governance issue, continues Houry, speaking as the country buckles under the weight of what the World Bank has called the worst economic collapse experienced in any nation for more than two centuries.

> The general state of impunity has been existent in Lebanon since the end of the civil war. The end of the conflict was buried within the Amnesty Law, which was supposed to be just about amnesty for past crimes but in fact it was used by the ruling class – most of them were warlords – almost as a blank cheque for the future.

> During the time I was running Human Rights Watch in Lebanon [from the mid noughties to the mid 2010s] you couldn't even hold a local police officer who tortured detainees accountable because they were [he was] being protected. They would say, 'Why are you punishing this guy? There is someone else who did something else. We're not going to punish everyone; we're not going to punish anyone.'

> There are a bunch of warlords [running Lebanon] but there are six dominant ones. They range from all sects, from the Shia side, to some of the Christian warlords, to some of the tycoons who came to power.

> The governance structure in Lebanon is such that it has a parliament, prime minister and president. But actually the key decisions since 2009 have always been made only

by about six men. If they cannot reach consensus then the system gets blocked.

Initially the idea of the Amnesty Law was to make civil peace but ultimately it's become an excuse for not governing. In practice it introduced this notion of impunity and once it was introduced, it was almost like a cancer that metastasized.

Human Rights Watch and another right-based NGO, Legal Agenda, began fighting back, spearheading a legal activism of which Lebanon had no heritage but which it has in recent years become increasingly recognised for.

Lebanon, like most Francophone countries, doesn't have a long tradition of judicial activism such as that seen in India, for example. We never had that in Lebanon, judicial review was not part of the activist trail here.

However since the 2010s, the local courts have become a field of battle for rights issues – rights of migrant domestic workers, rights of refugees.... Legal activists increasingly tried to use local courts to push back on these forms.

At Human Rights Watch, we started to analyse court cases a lot more systematically. In Lebanon, you can't even access all of the court cases as they are not even indexed electronically, so there was not much of a tradition of doing so.

Houry points to 'pioneers' Legal Agenda as even more influential than Human Rights Watch in cultivating legal activism in the country. I caught up with Legal Agenda's president Lama Karame, who for two years directed the NGO's strategic litigation work

'Legal activists have been at the forefront of social justice battles in the last two decades in Lebanon,' Professor Karame tells me.

They have successfully mainstreamed a culture and discourse centred on human rights, particularly in cases involving vulnerable and marginalised populations such as LGBT individuals, refugees, drug users, and domestic workers.

We have fought for and achieved important legal victories... been at the forefront of enacting significant laws that address previously overlooked issues, such as legislation guaranteeing the right to know the fate of missing and forcibly disappeared persons, as well as bills aimed at protecting women from domestic violence.

Legal activists have also pushed for progressive interpretations of existing laws. Through strategic litigation cases, legal activists have successfully obtained favourable rulings challenging the application of Article 534 of the penal code, which criminalises sexual conduct 'contrary to nature' and has historically been used to prosecute LGBT individuals.

These rulings have asserted that the provision should not be applied to same-sex intercourse, marking a significant step towards protecting the rights of the LGBT community in Lebanon. Landmark cases relating to the right to form syndicates, the right to maritime public property, and personal freedoms have also been pursued, shaping [a revived] legal landscape in the country.

Currently, many lawyer groups are actively engaged in bringing anti-corruption cases to court and others continue to litigate against banks. While there are challenges and limitations to bringing social change through judicial channels, there have been many tangible legal victories that have succeeded in fuelling popular and political support for controversial issues.

Beyond the direct involvement of lawyers, legal activists have also played a crucial role in discrediting the regime's rhetoric. They have mainstreamed legal knowledge and made it accessible to the public, removing it from the grip of experts and technocrats. By doing so, they have contributed to shaping the agenda of the protests [large uprisings erupted in 2015 and 2019], exposing the regime's attempts at hollow reforms and dangerous legislation.

Understanding of the law is no longer confined to legal experts. Legal advocates have succeeded in bridging the artificial gap between law and society, transforming law into a tool of social mobilisation.

Karame aligns with Houry in recognising the Beirut port blast as a tragedy among many that have bled out of Lebanon's entrenched system of impunity.

There have been numerous challenges faced by Lebanese people which can be grouped under the umbrella of impunity. The current financial crisis – a devastating impact of a Ponzi scheme orchestrated by the financial oligarchy – has caused people to lose all their savings and retirement plans.

The devaluation of the currency has left the entire public sector, the largest employer in the country, in crisis and unable to perform its basic duties. This has led to a semi paralysis of the state and its institutions, leading to a shortage in basic services and needs, and unsurprisingly, a new wave of emigration.

While ordinary Lebanese do not always see justice, those who remain are increasingly demanding it. The 'shift in expectations' represents arguably the biggest social change witnessed in the country, achieved as a result of growing awareness of rights and using the law to solve rather than create problems, according to Houry.

It's not fully linear but there is a line, a growing ecosystem with different stories of lawyers, activists, independent journalists and judges. A new system is slowly starting to take space.

'The idea that you kind of have a breakthrough and heads roll and you live happily ever after, that's not going to happen, that's clear. But we have to use almost guerilla-like tactics in the sense of approaching the issue of impunity from different angles. Wherever you can get small gains, you win them and you try to build momentum.'

CHAPTER TWENTY-THREE

ROADBLOCKS REIGN: ANTI-CORRUPTION PROTESTERS DEFEND ISRAEL

The train from Tel Aviv to Jerusalem felt dangerously airless on 13th February 2023. Pro-democracy supporters had been filling Kaplan Street in the country's financial capital every Saturday night since the start of the year. Now they were on their way to the city of the country's parliament and every carriage was packed full.

Every few miles the vehicle would stop unannounced, as if buckling under the weight of the extra passengers. It was 15 degrees, not a hot day, but without air conditioning or a cloud in the sky the sun pouring through the full length windows dried our mouths.

Parallel to our train tracks, we watched motorway traffic making the same journey south. Every vehicle seemed to have at least one blue and white national flag. Some cars and trucks had more hexagrams than doors.

Israel's new ruling coalition, the most right-wing government in its history, had been intending to vote through controversial reforms later in the day that would have removed judicial oversight of a government that had already come to be associated primarily with corruption and repression. The protesters descending on Israel's Knesset (parliament) and adjacent supreme court were determined to stop this happening.

Tamir Guy-Tsabary was among 80,000 pro-democracy activists making his presence felt that day, a mobilisation that saw the draft proposals postponed for the first time. The journey was not new to him. He routinely divides his time between the two cities, managing strategic collaborations in his day job at the *Jerusalem Post*.

'I am a father of three and I want my children to live in a democracy,' he explains. 'This is what is driving me. I was born in a democracy. They were born into a democracy. I want my life to end in a democracy and for them to prosper in a democracy.'

The word 'democracy' is used five times in this activist's staccato summary of his concerns. He goes on to reference 'democracy' by name on dozens more occasion across our 30-minute interview.

The analysis that democracy has been placed under threat by plans to strip judges of their legislation veto powers is 'justified', according to my second interviewee, a Senior Fellow at the Israel Democracy Institute.

Professor Gideon Rahat says centring campaign efforts around democracy alone, a word which is chanted repeatedly throughout the day, has been key to mobilising such large numbers over a sustained period. There are many LGBT rainbow flags at the rally, but it is not this community alone that is concerned by the implications of parliament being left unaccountable in a country that has no constitution, second house or tradition of presidential interventions.

'Gay people have their own interests in democracy,' Professor Rahat says. Women have their own... academia have their own too.... Many different groups have their specific reasons but they share the main reason. The success of the protest movement here has been to link all things under one roof, which is "democracy".'

There is a fairly festival-like atmosphere in the foothills in which Israel's parliament and supreme court are located on the day of the the movement's first major success – getting the reforms put on ice. Families picnic among the pine trees throughout an all-day occupation.

A national strike was organised on the day by the country's largest trade union. This was a 'bottom-up change', Rahat continues. '30,000 people have made a donation for the protests. 30,000 people is not trivial. In giving 100 shekels each they have raised 3 million shekels (825,000 dollars).'

The democracy movement also inspired unprecedented roadblocks. '100,000 people stood on the main highway: this is a miracle. One per cent of the population blocked Israel's main road. Translate it to the United States – that's 3 million people standing on Route 65.'

Rahat highlights the 'energy' created by the movement as turning the tide in the protesters' favour. When he says that the resultant impact on the economy was pivotal in swaying Prime Minister Benjamin Netanyahu, on March 27th, to shelve his government's divisive reforms, I ask whether the roadblocks were superfluous as this latest strike was one of many being planned and carried out.

> I think everything goes together. There is this energy that was created. It's the vibe. The pressure created impressions among people who were looking at the economy. I hadn't seen such opinion polls for years. I don't remember a poll

[prior to this] in which Netanyahu dropped down from number one for voter preference for leading the country.

Opinion polls hurt legitimacy because the opinion polls mean that many voters of the government do not support the reforms. Let's imagine that a third of the people who voted for Netanyahu do not want the reforms – that also creates a pressure.

Rahat adds that, critically, the military also became 'synchronised' with public dissent and the economy. Some reservists refused to attend routine training drills following shortly after the February demonstrations outside parliament. 'People in the military began saying they were not prepared to serve in the military of a dictatorship.'

Social movements that win defections from security forces are 60 per cent more likely to succeed, research from political scientist Erica Chenoweth has found. The Harvard academic is also credited with establishing the so-called 3.5 per cent rule – the notion that no government can withstand a challenge of this proportion of its population without accommodating the movement (or disintegrating).

Both these rules were reaffirmed in Israel as its democracy movement played out in early 2023. The first member of the ruling coalition to crack and concede he would not vote for the reforms was the government's defence minister.

'We don't have any checks and balances in Israeli politics other than the Supreme Court, Rahat reiterates. 'We don't have a strong constitution that can't be changed easily and that's exactly what the Knesset were doing, changing it easily. The leaders in the military consider the reforms a threat to a democracy and they are absolutely right, it has been a threat to democracy.'

While the judicial reforms were being pushed, Prime Minister Netanyahu was facing prosecution for bribery and fraud, with many drawing a connection between the two events.

'If people believe Israel is not a democracy, then we are not playing the game. Our defence minister, Yoav Gallant, felt the pressure within the military. You cannot run a military with divisions in it and he understood this for two reasons. First, because he had been a general. And second, because people who fought with him told him that he should resist, demonstrating near his house.'

Among the many vivid moments from Israel's democracy demonstrations were the scenes of protesters making their points with megaphones outside the houses of politicians' private addresses.

'The demonstrators shouted into the defence minister's house. "We fought together here and there and you have to listen to us – do not let them destroy democracy." These pressures, at the end of the day, they worked, because Gallant was socialised there, in the military. The other cabinet members, they didn't serve in the military.'

Netanyahu briefly fired his defence minister, only to reinstate him upon finally admitting his reforms faced defeat. In parking his coalition's plans, Netanyahu recognised in his backing-down announcement that there had been the potential for 'civil war'.

For protesters like Tamir Guy-Tsabary, who fought in the Israel-Lebanon wars, the worst case scenario of his country succumbing to conflict was avoided, while the vision to maintain democracy for his family returned into view.

Israel's anti-corruption movement remained at a crossroads as this book was being finalised. But the momentum had shifted in the protesters' favour prior to the Black Saturday attacks at the Supernova music fesitval, afterwhich protests were paused. The turnaround hadn't come easily. It involved direct action as well as the strategic framing of the message and the support of the military.

'When Netanyahu was due to visit Italy, we blocked the road to the airport,' Guy-Tsabary recalls. 'We did it because a demonstration that doesn't have the media covering it, without the protest becoming a story, does not lead to people understanding [what is at stake].'

'But we have never been the "anarchists" some wanted us to be. Not one single bottle was ever thrown. One thing we always said was that we would never resort to violence. It would have been the easiest thing in the world to smash the windows of banks and businesses. But we would never let anyone drag us down to that. Our focus was to show that we could be civilised and peaceful and yet as powerful as can be."

CHAPTER TWENTY-FOUR

SUNFLOWERS AND UMBRELLAS: TOWERING TAIWAN DELIVERS HOPE FOR HONG KONGERS

'I do not attribute blame to Joshua Wong, his personality or strategy – he is stronger perhaps than many social movement leaders in Taiwan.'

I am in discussion with a Taiwanese doctor of political science who, through his role as an NGO director, now works tirelessly in supporting Hong Kong's defeated student protesters to realise new residency some 200km (65 miles) away, on the main island of Taiwan. Bin-Jou Liao has supported thousands who rebelled against Beijing's creeping repression to navigate access to forms of residency in Taiwan, enabling breathing space from the fear of extradition to mainland China and potential prosecution for their protests.

Hong Kong's social movement against Beijing began in earnest in 2012 under Joshua Wong, a teenage activist. At just sixteen years old, Wong and his classmates conceived a movement they named Scholarism, convening a rally of 100,000 people, mostly young students, in defiance of Beijing plans to impose 'national education' on the city of Hong Kong.

China had previously established the notion of 'one country; two systems' for the transitional governance of Hong Kong until 2047. This followed the British handover to China in 1997.

Wong has been jailed several times for his activism since reaching adulthood. He writes in his prison diaries of a disdain for Beijing's strategy of 'legislating patriotism'. The sentiment was widely shared and expressed in Hong Kong during the 2010s, galvanised primarily through Wong's impassioned calls for democracy.

Wong, having mobilised his country's youth, upset all reasonable expectations and succeeded in his campaign against national education.

Wong then pushed for more.

China's government, the Chinese Communist Party (CCP), favoured governance compromised of a Beijing-appointed Chief Executive of Hong Kong. In addition, the CCP believed in a largely appointed, rather than elected, council of law-makers. The CCP blueprint for the council also entailed a mandate to appoint judges.

In 2014, Scholarism – a precocious activist collective who remained in their teens – drafted a plan to reform Hong Kong's electoral system. Scholarism pushed for universal suffrage to be integrated into the 'one country; two systems' model.

What followed was perhaps the most seismic and cinematic stand-off seen in social movements this century. Its scale may not have matched the Arab spring or others protests such as those seen in Israel in 2023. But the 'Umbrella Movement' – the confrontation of thousands of student protesters wielding umbrellas while resisting police discharging pepper spray in Hong Kong's parkour-esque battleground of skyscrapers and escalators – became a 79-day drama unlike anything we have seen before or since.

At least, that's how many of us consumed the Umbrella Movement. Hong Kong captured the international media's imagination in 2014 more than any other event, and so it reached living-rooms around the world.

However, that same year students in Taiwan, with far less international exposure, were embarking on their own audacious steps towards defying Beijing. The 'Sunflower Movement' saw 1,000 students occupy parliament to block a trade pact with the CCP. Protesters believed the deal would both hurt Taiwan's economy and leave it vulnerable to political pressure from Beijing in the future.

A florist contributed 1,000 sunflowers to the students outside the Legislative Yuan building. The sunflower was also an allusion to the country's Wild Lily Movement in 1990. Back then, a student sit-in resulted in Taiwan securing the right to direct elections similar to those craved in Hong Kong.

The lily is a symbol of freedom in Taiwan, whereas the sunflower resonates as an icon of hope, bending heliotropicaly towards the sun.

I have sought out my interviewee, Bin-Jou Liao, for some perspective in comparing the success of the Sunflower Movement with the failure of the Umbrella Movement. Besides having to shelter from Taiwan's latest typhoon arrival on the day we speak, Bin-Jou is perfectly placed to deliver some context.

Legally speaking, the sunflower student protesters truly violated our laws. But their action was the very definition of civil disobedience: your actions are against the law, but you believe in the 'higher law' sitting above law derived from a constitution or a government's action or an executive order.

We are lucky that the sunflower protesters, our protectors, picked a moment in time when they could succeed. By 2014, we had built a tradition of protest and democratisation over 30 years but in Hong Kong there's no tradition.

The concept of students occupying a parliament building for three weeks and ultimately winning concessions on legislation without reproach still feels exceptional, I suggest.

'As a general rule, even in Europe, student movements can't [play out in the same way]. Historically, we saw that in 1968 [when revolution in France was responded to through emergency elections]. And I know that in Western society today, in Britain and Germany for example, political leaders would invite students to dialogue before an occupation was attempted.'

Bin-Jou argues that the regional democracy movement 'peak' in 2014 came too early for Hong Kong, but was perfectly timed for Taiwan's protesters, who persuaded their leaders through their sit-in that ruling-without-compromise no longer fit.

'Our president in 2014, Ma Ying-Jeou, did not invite the students to dialogue before the occupation of parliament. It must have been grounded in authoritarian thinking. His thought process must have been: "Something has happened; a social movement has happened; you must react very strongly and very firmly." His pro-China policy became even more strong but from this rose much more dissatisfaction, so the movement was able to succeed. Ma Ying-Jeou handled things very badly.'

The way the Wild Lily movement had been managed by politicians in Taiwan in 1990, when student voices were accommodated, meant that Ma Ying-Jeou's resistance in 2014 exposed him to criticism from other politicians in Taiwan as being out of step with modern Taiwanese governance principles around being open to challenge.

Ultimately, the Taiwanese government's response to the Sunflower Movement became open to dialogue and negotiation. Eventually, a series of public hearings and a review of the trade agreement with the CCP were conducted, leading to its rejection.

In contrast, the Hong Kong government's response to the Umbrella Movement was marked by a refusal to make concessions and a tougher stance, resulting in the dismantling of protest sites on roadways and around the legislature. Elected (as opposed to appointed) representation on the legislative council dropped to under 25 per cent in 2023. The imposition of a national security law in 2021 has seen Wong face further spells in jail and 1million Hong Kong dollar (£100,000) arrest warrant bounties placed on the heads of his former comrades, now living in exile in Britain, Canada and the US.

The Sunflower Movement focused on grass roots mobilisation, drawing support from diverse segments of society including students, activists, academics, and various civil society organisations. It emphasised inclusivity and encouraged broad-based participation.

In addition to harnessing social media well, as all other effective protests had by now been doing, the movement organised persuasive public forums and assemblies. These often took place on the streets around the parliament. Participants and ordinary citizens had the opportunity to express their opinions, ask questions and engage in dialogue with each other.

The Sunflower Movement's primary demands were for a more democratic process and increased transparency in policy-making.

Many participants feared that the trade agreement could lead to increased economic dependence on China and undermine Taiwan's autonomy.

Students also highlighted broader social justice issues, including income inequality, labour rights and environmental concerns. While some participants were motivated by a simple aversion to China, there were also individuals who recognised various underlying concerns ranging from class divides to matters of the environment.

The Sunflower Movement left a legacy of political awakening and participation among Taiwan's younger generation. Some of the student protesters later became involved in political movements, with a portion joining the Democratic Progressive Party and gradually emerging as prominent young politicians over the next five to ten years.

Others participated in the establishment of new political parties, including the left-leaning, pro-independence New Power Party and Taiwan Statebuilding Party, as well as the Taiwan People's Party, which pushes ideology claiming 'All parties are equally bad.'

The Sunflower Movement's push for greater citizen participation led directly to local elections in the second half of 2014 including 'participatory budgeting' – where citizens choose what government budgets are spent on – in their political platforms, progressing democracy in a way that has since been recognised and emulated in over 1,500 cities around the world. Poe Yu-ze Wan, one of participatory budgeting's most influential pioneers, tells me it emerged in Taiwan as a 'convergence of two trends: deliberative democracy and community development'.

While participatory budgeting stands as the largest social legacy internationally, bequeathed by the Sunflower Movement, politically the movement highlighted and reinforced Taiwan's distinct identity, separate from China. It emphasised the importance of maintaining Taiwan's democratic values, sovereignty, and independence, resonating with many Taiwanese people and shaping ongoing discussions on national identity.

There has since been an increasing recognition of the 'China factor' and its impact on Taiwan across various aspects, including international relations, diplomacy, military, media, culture, and of course elections.

Taiwanese elections are primarily fought between the Democratic Progressive Party (DPP) and the Chinese Nationalist Party. The DPP now features amongst its parliamentarians some protesters who occupied parliament during the Sunflower Movement, such as the fearless digital minister Audrey Tang, who has become an admired international figure for her straight-talking on sensitive geo-political issues.

'Hong Kongers in Taiwan fear the Chinese Nationalist Party because they are much more pro-China and anti human rights than the DPP that have ruled in recent years, but they are also very disappointed in the DPP,' Bin-Jou tells me. While studying for his political science degree he became director of policy and research at an NGO founded in 2020 in response to the political situation in Hong Kong. His organisation is called 'Taiwanese civilian aid to HKers'.

'So many Hong Kongers in Taiwan are very disappointed with the DPP because their victory in the 2020 presidential election was married to the issues related to protecting Hong Kongers. The President Tsai Ing-Wen said she was anti-communist and for human rights: "We stand with human rights"' she said.'

Disappointment stems from the DPP's hesitancy to pass legislation delivering clarity on how Hong Kong student protesters – who have fled to Taiwan in their tens of thousands fearing arrest for participation in activities such as sit-ins in squares and roadways – can secure an indefinite right to remain in Taiwan.

Bin-Jou explains that Taiwan cannot classify Hong Kong entrants as refugees under its constitution, delicately maintained with mainland China. 'This is because Taiwan is still in a civil war with the Chinese Communist Party, so in that context Hong Kongers are not foreigners. They are neither foreigners nor citizens.'

'While countries like Canada and Britain have created laws to support refugees from Hong Kong, Taiwan cannot. It is not possible for our legislators. There is a classification of "protectors" – rather than refugees – which has been granted to some 2,000 student protesters that have come from Hong Kong to Taiwan.'

Bin-Jou's organisation is the primary source of information for the Hong Kong student protesters who need recognition as 'protectors'. The number of successful applicants so far is very few because they have to pass the review of the government and the review process is very strict [as well as vague in its criteria]. Bin-Jou estimates that the success rates in applying for standard short-term immigration residency instead are ten times higher. However in pursuing that route, the long-term future remains unresolved.

> They stayed here for one year or for two years. But then many flew out of Taiwan, to Britain and Canada. Our government policy and laws are not very clear and through this they show their negative attitude to Hong Kongers in Taiwan. It is because the DPP have to face the electorate as a whole and not just their own voters, of whom the younger ones are in support of Hong Kongers because of our social and cultural ties. The young from both countries

have always travelled back and forth and the connections among both cultures are there.

The DPP has younger voters who are pro-human rights but overall the party defines itself primarily as Taiwanese nationalists; they do not allow greater privileges or rights to Hong Kongers. So the DPP government's policy towards Hong Kongers has been very conservative and it creates a very difficult situation for Hong Kongers in Taiwan.

I don't dare to give hope to Hong Kongers coming to Taiwan. We just do what we can do to help those student protesters to find a way to live in Taiwan and support the creation of applications to government. Our role is restricted. We help with accessing the relevant contacts in government and we share with them information to help them live in Taiwan. But the ultimate responsibility falls with the government. If the government don't want to pass a very clear law and don't have a very clear policy to Hong Kongers in Taiwan, the problem is insolvable – we cannot solve the ultimate insecurity problem facing Hong Kongers seeking residency, so we are always very sad.

Bin-Jou is bashful when I encourage him to reflect on some of the contributions his organisation has made to the lives of Hong Kongers to date. He needs some prompting.

But his eyes lift again when he begins describing the support that has been provided to the student protesters from Hong Kong to at least resume their studies in Taiwan and to graduate.

We are dedicated to helping and protecting the students. Every semester we give scholarship fees for students in difficult economic situations. Fundraising for donations for our organisation is very difficult but we always managed to provide scholarships to those who needed it.

We also hear often about the students' psychological situations because those who suffered from the crackdown on protesters in Hong Kong have PTSD (post-traumatic stress disorder). Most of them need psychological counselling. Always, we arrange psychological counselling for them.

We collaborate with other organisations for the protesters, so they do not need to be involved with services affiliated in any way with the Hong Kong affairs. These organisations that we find for mental health support and other support are within Taiwanese society, not connected to Hong Kong.

And we have always helped, in the times when the Hong Kong government – or China's government – is pressuring for surveillance of Hong Kongers that is tight and high... with rescue missions: rescues for Hong Kong protesters to fly to Taiwan. It's very difficult because we have to have communication with our national security unit but we collaborate for Hong Kongers to fly to Taiwan's airports and for access then to enter into Taiwan.'

Bin-Jou concedes that just as the Sunflower Movement protesters were pre-occupied with maintaining a status-quo relationship between China and Taiwan, that one single issue continues to dominate Taiwan's entire governance agenda, to the detriment of Hong Kongers. There has simply been no meaningful space created for 'protecting the protectors' from Hong Kong.

The work of supporting Hong Kongers has been outsourced to NGOs but because government policy is inactive, we can't do more than we are doing. Our youth regards Taiwan as very advanced on human rights relative to elsewhere in Asia but that has not been tested while we've been a homogeneous society.

Once Hong Kongers or Chinese have come into Taiwan, the experience has been shown sometimes to be xenophobic. We have a very good human rights record and reputation internationally. But we have more to do. That is our challenge – our government's challenge; our society's challenge.

MOVEMENT: REFLECTIONS

What changed? Plenty, this past decade: the decade of disruption.

Who would have thought, ten years ago, reproductive rights would reach the largely staunchly Catholic Republic of Ireland? As recently as 2017, just one in four voters identified as pro-choice.

Who would have thought that Theresa May would legalise cannabis, for medicinal use?

In both instances, humanising the argument changed the conversation.

Savita Halappanavar, the pregnant dentist denied an abortion, had been left to die in Ireland under the terms of the constitution. This tragedy occurred despite miscarrying, buckling from back pain and going into septic shock. Her tale was the story of many mothers who had come before, but theirs had not been given a human face in the same way.

Billy Caldwell was not the first or only infant with epilepsy suffering a hundred brain seizures a day, episodes that could be averted with access to medicinal cannabis. But again, the victimhood of policy neglect now had a face, an identity.

Drug reform campaigners Volteface knew that they could win the argument by leaning into the morality. Rarely does a charity show the bravery to put a beneficiary through the jeopardy of breaking the law, as Volteface did. But like Billy's mum, they knew that by exposing inhumanity through a human story, politicians would be compelled to back down.

In declaring possession of Canadian-sourced medicinal cannabis to customs at an airport with a press conference pre-assembled, Volteface were following tactics that had been shown to work in other jurisdictions. They did their international homework, then got the law changed. The legacy is improved quality of life experienced by more than 20,000 people.

Charlotte Caldwell, Billy's mum, was equally as responsible as the charity she collaborated with. And throughout this book we've seen many mothers make movements, well, move.

Our anthropologist in Brazil credits mother-led associations there with giving children born with the Zika virus full and normal lives, no longer at risk of being defined by bio-identities.

In America, it's again mothers – women – who have led Black Lives Matter to become a fundraising phenomenon, drawing well over 100 million dollars in donations. Once more, the movement was ignited by a succession of human stories. But at this foundation there are stories behind the stories. The evidence base built by BLM around the return on investment generated by funding cultures of care has seen a succession of schools cancel their contracts with militarised police departments.

Schools are changing in the UK, too. Not least Montpelier High, formerly known as Colston Girls' School. The students there used to be taught to celebrate slave trader Edward Colston. Now the pupils are in charge of making sure the education delivered in their classrooms and across Bristol is grounded in the truth. The movement didn't end with a statue being thrown into the docks, that's purely the moment when it began in earnest.

Students the world over have shown that age need not be a barrier to the making of a movement. Teenager Joshua Wong pushed back on China's 'legislating of patriotism', audaciously succeeding in his campaign to block the imposition of a Chinese national curriculum in Hong Kong. While Wong and his Scholarism movement were ultimately met with a torrent of repression capable of terrosing any number of umbrellas, Taiwan continues to bend to the sun like the sunflowers synonymous with the student movement staged there in 2014.

For Taiwan's movement, timing was everything. The country's approach to inclusive governance had evolved steadily. Taiwan was ready in a way that Hong Kong was not. The challenge now is for Taiwan to continue creating space, moving forwards, to protect its brothers and sisters displaced from Hong Kong.

In Sweden, there may not be as many students descending on parliament square every Friday to 'school strike' for an environmentally sustainable future as there once were. But still they come. And their resistance more widely is taking on new forms.

Aurora have been advised they stand every change of succeeding in the legal action they have taken against the state. More than 200 such actions have been pursued worldwide by climate activists, with victories in France, Germany and the Netherlands achieving the highest profile. A template has been created that can and will be emulated by other movements.

Greta Thunberg, no longer a student, has pledged to continue to show solidarity with school children striking on Fridays. But she's now making her argument in other ways too. Arrested in Germany at the start of 2023, she faced criminal charges in Sweden later in the year after an oil tanker blockade.

Swedish press covering the trial backed Greta's direct action, the leader of Reclaim the Future told me, a position the group had never observed their country's mainstream media take before. Nacka, the Swedish province targeted by one of the group's most recent blockades, has pledged to disinvest in oil in the years since Greta first emerged onto the world stage.

Many of Sweden's young movement makers took part in school strikes earlier in their activism journey. Some are also former members of Extinction Rebellion (XR) Youth.

Environmental movements are influencing each other and in many cases they are converging. Aurora's legal adviser told me they see a role for direct action just as much as they see a role for student strikes and of course the strategic litigation approach they are prioritising over the next few years.

XR and Just Stop Oil are making progress in many areas, though not as quickly as the climate emergency demands. Banks are increasingly turning their backs on fossil fuel investment and the majority of political parties in the UK have signalled similar shifts. The party of government appears less persuaded, ahead of elections. This reinforces XR's calls for citizens' assemblies of the type that have brought gains for societies in Ireland and elsewhere.

This book has shown how the likes of Ireland and Taiwan have moved forwards through consciously harnessing progressive, participative democracy models. However we've also seen in these pages how democracy has been threatened in Israel through challenges to the rule of law. It remains to be seen how things will play out in western Jerusalem but the defence of democracy there has been designed in ways that protest movements the world over are likely to analyse further. The demonstrations have been about everything from LGBT+ rights to anti-corruption, but the umbrella word 'democracy' is credited with achieving the scale of the mobilisation: hundreds of thousands of people on successive Saturday nights across weeks and months.

Among those to attend the democracy protests in Israel this year was one of the interviewees I spoke to for my chapter on hacktivism, Sergey Shykevich. Like the others I met with for that section, he was gloomy about the direction hacktivism is headed, pointing to the growth of state-sponsored hacks. Private hackers, driven by the ethics outlined so eloquently by author Maureen Webb, have been discouraged by the authoritarian criminalisation of their campaigns. We've seen that in Iran at least, the creativity and contribution of hacktivists remains as inventive as ever, puncturing the perception of invincibility that underpins repressive regimes.

In Albania, we heard how museums have leant into their country's past reputation for repression, doing so deliberately, to historicise the association. Soft power is a tactic that Albania is sticking to in its patient pursuit of European Union membership.

While Albania cosies up to the Union, the Kremlin and its "special military operation" continues to cast a long shadow across the continent as a whole, within and beyond the borders of Ukraine. Performances from Belarus Free Theatre, bringing the *Dogs of Europe* book to the stage, showed how a Russian super state could play out by 2049 if blind eyes continued to be turned to the 'new Reich'.

The value of tapping into imagination is a prevailing theme of this book, whether that's envisioning worst case scenarios or painting pictures of how the world and its countries could be run better.

We need creatives like Belarus Free Theatre to show us what we're facing before it's too late, so that we can act; move.

We need creatives in contexts of censorship too. Adekan's street art shows us how truth can continue to be told in Turkey, despite it entering a post-media state.

Artistic intervention delivers many gifts. The work of art therapists Hospital Rooms illustrates this, as I witnessed on my visit to the medium-secure hospital, which will remain unnamed under the terms of the access. The mental health, prospects, goals and self-esteem of patients have all been bolstered by the mentorship of artists from the Hospital Rooms charity.

Traditional mental health therapists – counsellors – continue to drive transformations, sometimes bigger even than those in the individuals they treat. International Alert's psychosocial work countering the risk of traumatised individuals falling vulnerable to recruitment from the likes of Boko Haram and Islamic State is testament to that.

In Palestine, I witnessed how *sumud* – resilience – can also be reinforced through self-expression. Whether the Wall Museum can be credited or not with changing the actions of checkpoint guards towards women and girls, certainly it has strengthened the outlook and opportunities of story author participants such as Yara, the daughter of the Wall Museum's founder.

Peace and freedoms for Palestinians remains elusive. It can seem that it will always be so, living in intractable conflicts. It felt that way in Colombia too. The lessons shared with me from Bogota, from the man responsible for delivering the promises of the accord, was that peace can be realised if the agreement is un-limited and inclusive when the demands of all sides are written up. And crucially, the delivery plan must be structured to be carried out across four or five terms of government, whichever party is in power. This was corroborated by the metrics analyst I spoke to in Medellin, insisting the path to peace remains on track to be fully realised by the late 2030s.

The late 2030s? That timeline will feel a long time away for many Colombians. It is, of course. Social change is not always fast. And it is not always linear.

The Russian rights activists – legal rights trainers and games designers along with journalists and lawyers – carried a confidence their country was changing and challenge-able when I met them in Moscow and Saint Petersburg just a few short years ago. It could not be foreseen – expect perhaps by readers of *Dogs of Europe* – that they would be driven out of their country following the arrival of the full-scale war and the doubling-down on censorship that came with it.

For now, many Russians continue their work from outposts in central Europe and elsewhere. They are educating their compatriots still at home in ways to defend themselves in the courts against mistreatment inflicted through the perpetuation of corrupt systems. The skills taught by the activists are now more important than ever. The commitment and bravery shown is peaking also.

Laws are there to solve problems, not create them, the barrister of Carles Puigdemont, Gonzalo Boye, told me. That hasn't always been the case in Spain or its 'minority nations' of Catalonia and the Basque Country. But the fight is becoming fairer. Juries are more widely used. Both regions have more autonomy and prosperity than they had. ETA has disarmed. Boye told me each region's movements also now possess more legitimacy than they had and that their opponents now have, achieved through the sovereigntists' commitment to non-violent resistance.

In Lebanon too, its the campaigners rather than those championing the status quo who now hold all the legitimacy. Like in Spain, an era of lazy amnesty has passed its expiry date. 'Expectations have been changed' through the success of strategic litigation brought and pursued with resilience by groups including Legal Agenda and Human Rights Watch. Case law has now been established supporting everything from LGBT+ rights to the remembering of the disappeared.

The work of legal activists in Lebanon has seen changes hard won. But change does not always come by design. In the Gulf, the blending of family and individual approaches to decision-making – which stands to support individual rights, freedoms and opportunities in the long term – appears to be happening organically, through forces detached from protest or politics. It appears unlikely that movement in Qatar could have been catalysed by design, but that hasn't prevented it from starting to happen.

Techniques for change, when they can be identified and applied, can nonetheless become corrupted. Approaches to software and communications can be manipulated for harm as well as social benefit, as we've seen in Ethiopia.

It's elsewhere in East Africa, however, that this book has arguably seen its most timely and needed manifestation of social change. The East African Community (EAC), a growing economic coalition of countries, is showing global leadership in embracing the benefits that can be brought about by softening borders. Refugees from EAC countries can now claim the rights of citizens in any other nation within the bloc. This includes the freedom of movement and the right to work.

From Ukraine to Palestine to Sudan, this book reminds us that while stories of social change are being realised all over the planet, wars and conflict are not going away. Social movements will increasingly be required across borders, not merely within them

The change in approach towards refugees in East Africa is down to economics as much it is down to internationalism or empathy. As documented earlier in this publication, the EAC policy was implemented following World Bank research which concluded that increased overall average local income and employment in Kenya's Turkana county was attributable to the Kakuma refugee camp established there.

Nevertheless, the shift demonstrates the imagination, independent thought and optimism fundamental to all social change movements.

Through international curiosity, vision and application, disruptors will continue to move societies forward in the decades to come. Solidarity and shared leadership of a style we've seen in Sweden will be crucial for swerving burnout in the battles ahead.

And as they say in Freetown Christiania, change is most often realised when we don't stop, or wait, to be granted permission.

ACKNOWLEDGEMENTS

Thank you to Martin Hickman for your support of the 'chasing social change' concept and your commitment shown to me as a first-time book author. I had no desire to speak to any other publisher once we'd had our first conversation. You have been so straightforward to work with, so clear, accommodating and generous. Thank you also to Gaby Monteiro, Richard Williams and all at Acropolis and Canbury Press.

Thank you to all my interviewees for the lessons you've shared, alternative yet evidenced pathways to change.

Many thanks to *New Internationalist*, *openDemocracy*, *UnHerd* and *Mental Health Today* for granting permission to re-publish extracts from articles I'd previously had published on their pages. Similarly, thanks to *International Alert* for allowing material previously posted on their blog site to be republished in this book.

Thank you to all the editors who support independent and constructive journalism, freelance writing and reporting.

Thank you Nadine for your faith, enthusiasm and encouragement. I am glad you were the person I first shared this idea with. You made it seem a far more manageable marathon. Thank you Hannah for helping me with the title, for your writing, your wisdom, your humour and values. Thank you Chloe for always helping me think everything through, untangling the knots.

Jasmine, my patient assistant on reporting trips across Sweden and the M-Shed Museum in Bristol, England, while still just sevenyears old. My daughter, my friend, you are the most joyful and tireless company I could ever ask for.

Thank you to those lost this year and all who have loved and are loved.

Thank you Heider Nasralla for normalising my plans to visit Palestine for the first time. I will never forget my experiences there, I am so glad I made the journey and I can't wait to return. Thank you Rani for your help in Bethlehem.

At *International Alert* I met so many people that remain grounding examples: Mariam, Olfa, Mary, Kim, Senait, Cindy, Caroline, Gemma, Jessica, Irina.

At *Transparency International*, thank you Ara, Gloria, Josie, Mohamed, Michael, Najla and Sara for being you.

Thank you Tunde and Mazin for seeing and sharing the light and the colour. You need to. I needed it too.

Thank you Theresa and Peter for faith, freedom and bravery.

Thank you Tunde #1, the boss and the bringer of everything that followed.

Simon, Lucy, Valerie, Patrick, Raj, Abi, Ollie, Debbie and Ella, thank you for your generosity.

Finally, thank you so much, Innocent, for being my adviser on this journey into book publishing – you unlocked everything in my mind and made me see what was possible.

FULL LIST OF INTERVIEWEES

- Roger Hallam, XR / Just Stop Oil co-founder
- George Hibberd, Just Stop Oil protester
- Dr Nick Anim, Transform Network Research Director and XR member
- Racquel Frescia, Sweden Fridays For Future co-ordinator
- Rahmina Paullete, Kenya Fridays for Future conservationist, COP26 Kenya representative and head campaigner at Let Lake Victoria Breathe Again
- Irma Kjellström, Reclaim the Future leader and spokesperson
- Ida Edling, Aurora leader, legal and scientific co-ordinator and spokesperson
- Inya Borre, Extinction Rebellion Sweden member
- Dr Elaine Daly – Lecturer at Blekinge Institute of Technology Strategic Leadership Towards Sustainability
- Kirsten Larsen, Freetown Christiania social anthropologist and spokesperson
- Cleo Lake, Countering Colston anti-racism campaign lead and former Mayor of Bristol
- Helen McConnell-Simpson, Curator of Social History at Bristol's M Shed museum

- Gulsan Kanat-Dinc, social worker at the Turkish women's refuge 'Purple Roof'
- Professor Mary Lou O'Hara, Director of Women and Gender Studies at Kader Has University, Istanbul
- Richael Carroll, National Convenor at ARC (abortion rights campaign), Ireland
- Paul North, Director of Volteface
- Amber Moore, Drugs Analyst and Research Manager at User Voice
- Three anonymised inpatients at a medium secure hospital in SE England and their support worker
- Yara van Teeffelen, Palestinian political design and interaction design graduate and her parents Toine and Mary Teeffelen, who contributed their story of Israeli police repression to the Wall Museum curated by Toine on the 'apartheid' wall separating Palestine and Israel
- Gonzalo Boye, lawyer of Catalan independence leader Carles Puigdemont, who has served eight years for an ETA kidnapping
- Mary Hwyere, Nigerian counsellor and peacebuilder in Borno State
- Oumar Arby; Malian peacebuilder in Bamako and Abuja
- Emilio Archila, lawyer responsible for implementation of the Colombia peace settlement
- Gerard Martin, Medellin-based peace monitor for the Kroc Institute
- Etleva Demollari, Albanian anti-communism protester turned Director of the House of Leaves Museum of State Surveillance
- Marsida Turku, a medical student who works in a second museum, BunkArt, that commemorates the victims of the Albanian dictatorship

- Sara Kureta, Albanian philosophy student
- Natalia Koliada, Belarus Free Theatre Director and human rights activist
- Galyna Sergeyeva, Ukrainian journalist
- Polina Fillipova, spokesperson for Russia's Sakharov Centre
- Anonymised Russian journalist at human rights / legal / journalism / gaming NGO Team 29
- Adekan, a Turkish street artist
- Anonymised Armenian museum supervisor at Istanbul's Orhan Pamuk 'Museum of Innocence'
- Sergey Shykevich, Cyber Threat Intelligence manager at Check Point Security
- Maureen Webb, a constitutional lawyer and author of *Coding Democracy – How Hackers Are Disrupting Power, Surveillance and Authoritarianism*
- Naomi Colvin, Director of the European NGO Blueprint for Free Speech
- 'Abraham', a web developer at a digital marketing start-up in Ethiopia
- 'Toler', Ethiopian economist, who like tech entrepreneur 'Abraham', lived through the 2016-2017 national state of emergency
- Marianna Maggi, Italian social worker
- Giovanna De Maio, foreign policy analyst at the Brookings Institute
- Alessandro Falcioni, spokesperson for Italian Catholic charity supporting refugees, 'Citizens of the World'
- Anonymised refugees sleeping rough in Rome and Kos
- Elli Xenou, a senior advocacy worker at the Athens branch of Doctors of the World

- Spyros Oikonomou, Greek Council for Refugees spokesperson
- Alysson Felix, the world's 'most medalled' sprinter and women's rights campaigner
- Salwar Eid Naser from Bahrain and Katerina Stefanidi, World Champion athletes from Bahrain and Greece
- Reem Meshal, Egyptian Professor of Middle Eastern Studies at Education City's Hamed Bin Khalifa University in Qatar
- 'Sara' and Aisha Al-Naama, Qatari women student interviewees on the country's gendered laws and customs
- Tamir Guy-Tsabary, Israeli democracy protester and strategic communications lead at the *Jerusalem Post*
- Professor Gideon Rahat, Senior Fellow at the Israel Democracy Institute
- Professor Parry Scott, Professor of Medical Anthropology at the Federal University of Pernambuco
- Cicley Gay, Chair of Black Lives Matter
- Nadim Houry, CEO of the Arab Reform Network and former founding Director of Human Rights Watch in Lebanon
- Professor Lama Karame, Director of Strategic Litigation at Legal Agenda
- Bin-Jou Liao, Taiwanese doctor of political science and Director of Research at Taiwanese Civil Aid to Hong Kongers
- Poe Yu-ze Wan, Professor of Sociology at National Sun Yat-sen University

Outside the House of Leaves, the Museum of Secret Surveillance, Tirana, Albania. © Barney Cullum

BARNEY CULLUM

Barney Cullum is a journalist and campaigns analyst focused on international social issues. He has reported on inventive forms of activism around the world for *New Internationalist*, *openDemocracy* and *UnHerd*. Raised in the creative city of Bristol in south west England, where he began his career as a features writer, his work has taken him from Brazil to Palestine to Russia. Barney has also worked as the media adviser to peacebuilders International Alert and led communications for anti-corruption campaigners Transparency International.

Publish with Us!

We specialise in memoir, biography, autobiography, history and business books,
but will consider other factual genres.

acropolispublishing.co.uk

contact@acropolispublishing.co.uk

Milton Keynes UK
Ingram Content Group UK Ltd.
UKHW012144131223
434291UK00003B/213